WOMEN, PRECARIOUS WORK AND CARE

Law, Society, Policy series

Series Editor: **Rosie Harding**,
University of Birmingham

Law, Society, Policy seeks to offer a new outlet for high
quality, socio-legal research monographs and edited
collections with the potential for policy impact.

Also available in the series:

Pandemic Legalities:
Legal Responses to COVID-19 – Justice and Social
Responsibility
Edited by **Dave Cowan** and **Ann Mumford**

Forthcoming in the series:

Deprivation of Liberty in the Shadows of the Institution
By **Lucy Series**

Find out more at
bristoluniversitypress.co.uk/law–society–policy

Law, Society, Policy

Series Editor: **Rosie Harding**,
University of Birmingham

Find out more at
bristoluniversitypress.co.uk/law-society-policy

EMILY GRABHAM

WOMEN, PRECARIOUS WORK AND CARE: THE FAILURE OF FAMILY-FRIENDLY RIGHTS

BRISTOL
UNIVERSITY
PRESS

First published in Great Britain in 2021 by

Bristol University Press
University of Bristol
1-9 Old Park Hill
Bristol
BS2 8BB
UK
t: +44 (0)117 954 5940
e: bup-info@bristol.ac.uk

Details of international sales and distribution partners are available at
bristoluniversitypress.co.uk

British Library Cataloguing in Publication Data
A catalogue record for this book is available from the British Library

ISBN 978-1-5292-1871-8 paperback
ISBN 978-1-5292-1872-5 ePub
ISBN 978-1-5292-1873-2 ePdf

Cover design: Andrew Corbett
Front cover image: Richard Drury/Getty Images

Printed and bound by CPI Group (UK) Ltd, Croydon, CR0 4YY

Contents

List of Figures

Acknowledgements

I would like to thank all the women interviewed as part of the project for giving their time and insights so generously to this research. Thank you to Ruth Cross and Jo Bird of USDAW and Julia Waltham and Rebecca Jones of Working Families for your support. Deena Ladd and Mary Gellatly from the Toronto Workers' Action Centre provided comparative and activist perspectives for which I am very grateful. This project has taken longer than anticipated due to chronic illness, and many people who provided their expertise at earlier stages of the project have moved on in their careers. Thank you to Sally Brett, Scarlett Harris and Hannah Reid (formerly of TUC), Sharon Greene (formerly Unison National Women's Officer) and Jonathan Swan and Liz Gardiner (formerly of Working Families).

Thank you to Diamond Ashiagbor, Lizzie Barmes, Nicole Busby, Joanne Conaghan, Katie Cruz, Ruth Dukes, Judy Fudge, Lydia Hayes, Claire Mummé and Emily Rose for your inspirational feminist perspectives on labour law and my colleagues at Kent Law School for providing an enriching community in which to work. For feedback on the project and this book, thank you to Donatella Alessandrini, Kate Bedford, Nicole Busby, Ruth Dukes, Ruth Fletcher, Judy Fudge, Jessica Grabham, Grace James, Suhraiya Jivraj, Karon Monaghan QC, Amanda Perry-Kessaris and Erika Rackley.

I am very grateful to Sarah Vickerstaff and Leah Vosko for generously mentoring the project. Thank you to Didi Herman and Toni Williams who, as heads of Kent Law School, helped me dedicate time to completing the project. Samenua Sesher has been instrumental in helping this book into the world through her insights and feedback. I am grateful to Rosie Harding for providing a home for this book in the Law, Society, Policy series of Bristol University Press, and to Helen Davis,

Senior Commissioning Editor for Law for her invaluable advice shepherding me through the reviews process. Detailed feedback from three anonymous reviewers improved the book significantly – thank you to these people for engaging so thoughtfully. Thank you also to Freya Trand and Millie Prekop for their patience in helping me finalize the book.

The Economic & Social Research Council generously funded the research that led to this book (ES/K001108/1).

Finally, more thanks than can ever be expressed to my partner Kate and our companions Olive, Nico and Goose.

Series Editor's Preface

The Law, Society, Policy series publishes high-quality, socio-legal research monographs and edited collections with the potential for policy impact. Cutting across the traditional divides of legal scholarship, Law, Society, Policy offers an inter-disciplinary, policy-engaged approach to socio-legal research which explores law in its social and political contexts with a particular focus on the place of law in everyday life.

The series seeks to take an explicitly society-first view of socio-legal studies, with a focus on the ways that law shapes social life, and the constitutive nature of law and society. International in scope, engaging with domestic, international and global legal and regulatory frameworks, texts in the Law, Society, Policy series engage with the full range of socio-legal topics and themes.

ONE

Introduction

It's a cold spring morning and Renuka and I are sitting in a coffee shop in Harrow. Renuka has agreed to be interviewed about her experiences of balancing zero-hours work in a high-street shop with caring for her two young children. We have been talking for nearly an hour. I say to her: "If you had to draw what it feels like to be doing what you are doing right now with work and with the kids, what would you draw?"

Renuka starts sketching. "It would be a headless chicken", she says. "I can't draw a chicken. I am just going to put a box and put 'chicken'". She draws the square outline of her chicken body and labels it 'Chicken's body'.

"These are my hands", she says, drawing stick arms out to each side. "These are my legs, because I am running". She draws clouds of dust under her stick feet to show speed.

"You are running quite fast there", I say.

"I need to juggle", Renuka says. "Meals. Work. And the reason I don't have a head is because it's filled with money worries and so it's not functioning".

The headless chicken sits for a moment on the page, with its speedy feet and boxes floating to either side. Renuka labels each of these boxes in turn: meals, work, children. Then we both pause and look at what she's created. Quietly, she draws another box, which hovers above the chicken's body like an empty rectangular halo. Renuka adds a label: 'money worries'.

"This", she says, pointing to the 'money worries' box, "is independent of what's going on here". She points to the body and hands. Only later, after I have asked her what her head

Figure 1.1: Renuka's sketch of a "headless chicken"

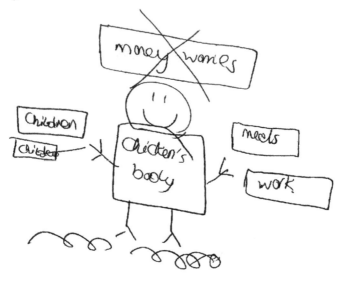

would look like if she didn't have money worries, does Renuka add the smiling face that we can see in Figure 1.1. "I'd still be running around", she says. "But I would be happy".

Renuka's story mirrors the experience of many women who balance precarious work with caring for their children or family members. Women are the majority of those on temporary, zero-hours and involuntary part-time contracts in the United Kingdom.[1] While most working parents experience problems juggling work and care, women in precarious work often worry about how to secure their next shift. Their jobs are not well suited to 'flexible work' or 'working from home' because the shifts are already last minute and the work requires them to be physically present – in a supermarket, for example. Since the COVID-19 pandemic, many of these women have been

---

[1] Women's Budget Group (2020) *Women, Employment, and Earnings: A pre-budget briefing from the UK Women's Budget Group.* Available at: https://wbg.org.uk/wp-content/uploads/2020/02/final-employment-2020.pdf

called 'key workers' for their role in keeping healthcare, care work, retail, delivery, public transport and education systems running effectively.[2] According to the Trades Union Congress (TUC), women are almost twice as likely as men to be key workers, and Black and minority ethnic workers are more likely than White workers to be in key worker occupations.[3] The research for this book took place prior to the COVID-19 pandemic, but its findings about precarious workers resonate strongly with emerging research on key workers.

People might ask why precarious workers do not draw on the growing range of family-friendly rights in managing conflicts between competing work and care priorities. The assumption might be that with such rights available, women who are struggling are to some degree responsible for their circumstances, due to their making poor choices about work or not managing their money well, for example. Drawing on interviews with women in precarious work, this book challenges such arguments.[4] Precarious jobs are not 'flexible' in a way that workers can find useful. These jobs often make it much harder, rather than easier, to balance work and care. The way that contracts are set up in precarious jobs tips the balance of power disproportionately in favour of employers. Precarious workers do not feel that they can negotiate flexible work for fear of being seen as unreliable by their employers and passed over for future shifts or contracts. Because their pay is often very low and fluctuates considerably, their priority is to secure ongoing income rather than reduce working hours.

During the pandemic, many women have faced significant problems covering the care for their children as schools have

---

[2]   TUC (2021) *Key workers: Decent pay and secure work for key workers through coronavirus and beyond.* Available at: https://www.tuc.org.uk/sites/default/files/2020-09/Key%20workers%20report.pdf

[3]   TUC (2021).

[4]   Many thanks to an anonymous reviewer for Bristol University Press for pointing out this argument.

closed, and as many as seven in ten requests for furlough have been turned down for working mothers.[5] Providing ongoing schooling for children of key workers has shown how essential care is to the economy, but it has not resolved problems for key workers in covering non-school hours. Workers without access to paid parental leave or flexible work have been forced to use annual leave, reduce their working hours or take unpaid leave in order to cope. As the TUC has put it, the combination of the pandemic and the narrow coverage of family-friendly rights has left many women facing the loss of their jobs or a 'catastrophic loss of income'.[6]

With these issues in mind, *Women, Precarious Work and Care* has two aims. The first is to describe in detail what life is like for women in precarious work, including key workers: their daily routines, care strategies and experiences at work as well as the financial and emotional stresses involved in balancing precarious work with a care responsibility. And the second aim is to draw on these insights to explain why precarious workers need a new approach to family-friendly rights, and what it could look like.

From 2015 to 2017, I conducted 33 in-depth interviews with women in precarious work across the mainland UK: Dundee, Glasgow, Durham, York, Leeds, Liverpool, Stoke-on-Trent, Manchester, Nottingham, Milton Keynes, Ebbw Vale and London. These women were from diverse ethnic backgrounds, held different kinds of precarious jobs in a variety of sectors and had different kinds of care responsibilities.[7] Many of the

---

[5] TUC (2021) *Working Mums: Paying the Price.* Available at https://www. tuc.org.uk/workingparents

[6] Ibid.

[7] See Appendix. Thirteen of the respondents defined their ethnicity as White, five as Asian, three as Black British, two as Black, two as White British, one as African Caribbean, one as 'mixed race', one as Brazilian, one as British Asian, one as Sri Lankan, one as Iranian and one was unknown. Most of the women were employed in retail, further and higher education, care and cleaning.

women were single parents. I interviewed them at their homes, walking to and from nurseries and schools to pick up children, in cafes or at their workplaces. Sometimes, like Renuka, they agreed to draw pictures to show how they felt about work and care, and these pictures provide important visual insights into their experiences. Research studies of this kind are useful when we need to understand the detail and context of people's lives: how much they understand of law, for example, and whether they feel confident in asserting legal rights.[8] After the interviews, I went back through the transcripts and sketches to draw out key themes within the context of these women's lives, thinking about how these women understood their contracts and the law. I found that women in precarious work face many problems that the current range of family-friendly employment rights simply do not recognize. This book explains my findings and points to some potential ways forward.

Family-friendly rights and precarious workers

The creation and expansion of family-friendly employment rights has been a very positive development for many working women and men in the UK over the past few decades.[9] These laws include rights to maternity and paternity leave and pay, shared parental leave and pay, the right to request flexible work

---

[8] Qualitative research studies of this kind are not directed at establishing statistical validity but aim to provide an account of complex interlocking issues, social context and people's motivations. See further Ritchie, J. and Lewis, J. (eds) (2013) *Qualitative Research Practice: A Guide for Social Science Students and Researchers*, California: Sage.

[9] For helpful guides to family-friendly rights, check the websites of the TUC (https://www.tuc.org.uk/workplace-guidance/family-friendly-work) and the organization Working Families (https://workingfamilies.org.uk/). Working Families has a telephone helpline for parents and carers – see their website for details.

and parental leave, for example.[10] Yet workers like Renuka do not fit in with the assumption underpinning family-friendly working on the whole, which is that the best way to balance work and care is for women to negotiate flexible work. Many precarious workers are not eligible for family-friendly employment rights in the first place because they are not classified as employees or have not been working for long enough with the same employer. So-called 'employment status' and 'length of service' criteria are often used as limits on people's eligibility for family-friendly rights, and these limits reflect an out-of-date approach to the world of work.[11]

Employment rights to family-friendly work patterns are based on the idea of a secure employee in a permanent, professional role needing adjustments to what is essentially a nine-to-five working routine – what's commonly called the 'standard employment relationship', or SER. The SER describes what many of us think is an ideal job: lifelong, full-time employment on a wage that is good enough to support a family. Policy makers still use the SER when determining who should receive employment rights. With big changes in economic production models and the world of work, however, the SER is now felt to be unstable.[12] Its ability to explain and respond to the rise of the

---

[10] For in-depth analysis of the history of family-friendly rights, see further James, G. and Busby, N. (2020) *A History of Regulating Working Families: Strains, Stereotypes, Strategies and Solutions*, Oxford: Hart Publishing.

[11] For example, the Women's Budget Group has pointed out that 28 per cent of women and men in employment cannot access rights to maternity and paternity pay because of employment status or insufficient length of employment. See further Women's Budget Group (2018) *Maternity, Paternity and Parental Leave: Briefing from the UK Women's Budget Group on the state of maternity, paternity and parental leave in the UK*. Available at: https://wbg.org.uk/wp-content/uploads/2018/10/Parental-leave-October-2018-w-cover-1.pdf

[12] See for example Fudge, J. (2017) 'The future of the standard employment relationship: Labour law, new institutional economics, and old power resource theory', *Journal of Industrial Relations*, 59(3): 374–92.

'gig economy', 'just-in-time' production models, outsourcing and precarious work is under question.[13] Precarious work, also termed 'vulnerable work', includes agency work, zero-hours contracts and temporary work, and it has attracted significant attention from the International Labour Organization as part of its Decent Work agenda.[14] If the types of work that people are doing do not look like SER jobs anymore, one question is how to make sure precarious workers and key workers still have the employment rights they need.

Another problem, however, is how to recognize unpaid care when designing employment rights.[15] Unpaid care refers to the work of sustaining others physically, emotionally and financially: children, for example, or elderly relatives. Caring for loved ones is economically, as well as socially, very important. This kind of care is predominantly performed by women.[16] Employment strategies and economic models – including the UK government's recent pandemic economic recovery plans – do not pay enough attention to unpaid care.[17] This is also a problem in employment law because the SER assumes

---

[13] For an ambitious and timely project investigating this question, see the European Research Council–funded WorkOD project led by Ruth Dukes: https://workondemand.co.uk/

[14] The International Labour Organization is the United Nations body that focuses on setting labour standards. For Decent Work, see further: https://www.ilo.org/global/topics/decent-work/lang--en/index.htm

[15] See Vosko, L. (2010) *Managing the Margins: Gender, Citizenship, and the International Regulation of Precarious Employment*, Oxford: Oxford University Press.

[16] Charmes, J. (2019) *The Unpaid Care Work and the Labour Market: An analysis of time use data based on the latest World Compilation of Time-use Surveys*, Geneva: International Labour Organization. Available at: https://www.ilo.org/wcmsp5/groups/public/---dgreports/---gender/documents/publication/wcms_732791.pdf

[17] See the House of Commons Women and Equalities Committee (2021) *Unequal impact? Coronavirus and the gendered economic impact,* fifth report of session 2019–21.

that a person's paid work will be performed in the absence of having to care for anyone else.[18] The very idea of a 'normal' full-time job assumes somebody other than the worker is doing the housework and looking after children and elderly parents. In this way, the combination of the rise in precarious work and the inadequate recognition of the unpaid care burden has led to significant problems in providing effective employment rights to many women.[19]

What this book argues

Renuka's experiences put her right in the middle of these big policy debates. Renuka's zero-hours job was precarious, and she was trying to do her job while caring for two young children. She spoke about running around like a headless chicken, worrying about money and putting food on the table for her children. She did not tell her employer about her need to balance work with care because she feared losing out on future shifts. She wanted to secure a better, permanent contract at work, and she wanted to show she was willing, so when her boss called with last minute shifts, she found the money for the bus and went in, whether it was convenient for her care arrangements or not.

This book argues for a new approach to family-friendly rights in the UK that is capable of recognizing the distinct

---

[18] See Conaghan, J. (2019) 'Gender and the Labour of Law' in H. Collins, G. Lester and V. Mantouvalou (eds) *Philosophical Foundations of Labour Law*, Oxford: Oxford University Press, pp 271–86; Fudge, J. (2011) 'Labour Law as a Fictive Commodity: Radically Reconceptualising Labour Law' in G. Davidov and B. Langille (eds) (2011) *The Idea of Labour Law*, Oxford: Oxford University Press, pp 120–36.

[19] See Fudge, J. and Owens, R. (2006) *Precarious Work, Women, and the New Economy: The Challenge to Legal Norms*, Oxford: Hart Publishing; Conaghan, J. and Rittich, K. (2005) *Labour Law, Work, and Family: Critical Perspectives*, Oxford: Oxford University Press.

experiences of precarious workers.[20] The core problem that women like Renuka face is that they have taken a contract structured to meet the employer's needs, often in circumstances where they have little choice in the work available. This needs to be understood in the broader context of what the legal scholar Ruth Dukes calls 'contracting for work' – the exchange of labour power for wages in a 'self-consciously legal act with important social dimensions'.[21] The precarious contract gives the manager a higher degree of control over the worker than other types of employment contract would do. Because the contract gives the manager discretion to allocate shifts (and, therefore, income), or renew temporary contracts, precarious workers need to make sure they can secure ongoing work. This significantly undermines their ability to mention their care responsibilities to managers or obtain family-friendly work patterns.

Over the course of the coming chapters, this book takes us on a journey through women's experiences of precarious work and care. Chapter Two focuses on how the women interviewed got into precarious work, following their pathways into zero-hours, agency, temporary and involuntary part-time work. Chapter Two also explores what these women did to make ends meet on fluctuating and often low incomes, because finances were an important reason why they avoided talking about care at work. Chapter Three then turns to the unpaid care that these women provided, focusing on women's daily routines of care, the impact of care on their social lives and their feelings about care. The interviewees reported being the 'coordinators' of care, arranging ongoing care around work in complex networks of other adults, nurseries, schools and care workers. For that reason, Chapter Four

---

[20] See in particular Fredman, S. (2004) 'Women at Work: The Broken Promise of Flexicurity', *Industrial Law Journal*, 33(4): 299–319.

[21] Dukes, R. (2019) 'The Economic Sociology of Labour Law', *Journal of Law & Society*, 46(3): 396–422.

picks up on the specific strategies that the interviewees used to set up and manage care networks around their precarious jobs and shows how the changing routines of such jobs had effects on wider groups of people.

Chapters Five, Six and Seven focus in on the employment relationship. In Chapter Five, I explore these women's feelings about their work and their employment status, finding that they feared reprisals for "rocking the boat" by mentioning care or asking for care-friendly working arrangements. This frames Chapter Six, which explores what happened when the interviewees could not avoid disclosing a care responsibility at work – and how employers responded. In Chapter Seven we see that many of the experiences highlighted in previous chapters – difficulties arranging care around work, feelings of being a 'second class citizen' or being overwhelmed by managing care around a precarious job – fed into women's 'bargaining power' at work. Bargaining power describes the relative power between employer and worker and helps explain why 'regular' approaches to family-friendly rights are not suitable for those in precarious work.

What can we do?

Renuka and the other women interviewed for this project deserve effective legal rights that redress the power imbalances caused by their precarious contracts and make it possible for them to balance care with work. This is all the more pressing for key workers who have risked their health and wellbeing to continue working in the midst of the pandemic. Chapter Eight presents seven key principles that could underpin new family-friendly rights for precarious workers. These include: supporting measures to outlaw precarious work; making employment status irrelevant for claiming care-friendly rights; aiming for 'care-friendly' work instead of 'flexible' work; focusing first on the care responsibility (rather than a person's employment status); increasing access to paid leave; ensuring rights from day one; and creating effective monitoring and enforcement mechanisms that do not leave it just to workers to enforce their rights.

In writing this book, it has been difficult to summarize the diverse experiences that women related to me over the course of those interviews. Wherever possible, I have related the detail of what women told me, using pseudonyms to help protect their identities. I am immensely grateful to each of the women for speaking to me when time was inevitably a precious resource for them. I still recall each interview, remember what it was like meeting each woman either in person or on the phone. The research has been slow, but I hope that it does justice to these women's experiences and provides a way of acknowledging their intelligence, ingenuity and hard work.

TWO

Starting and Surviving in Precarious Work

The point at which each of the women interviewed for this book entered precarious work in the first place was a crucial one for them. It shaped their ability to provide for themselves and their loved ones financially, and it set in motion a range of daily and weekly working and caring patterns with effects on wider networks of family and friends. This chapter explores these women's narratives of looking for work and starting precarious jobs.

It is often argued that women choose zero-hours or temporary contracts so as to allow them to better manage unpaid care alongside their jobs. The women on this study told a different set of stories. A common theme was lack of choice. These women did not opt for precarious work in a situation where they felt control over the jobs available to them. They chose zero-hours, temporary, or low-hours jobs because they needed the money and because there was a lack of other work available to them. There was evidence of structural racism affecting which jobs women could take on. Interviewees did not report negotiating over the terms and conditions of their jobs; indeed, as we will also see in Chapter Seven, they believed the power to decide about the types of jobs available and to set terms and conditions resided with the employer or manager. While women did find ways to assert themselves at work, they often could not negotiate care-friendly working patterns right at the outset of their employment. This meant they started their new job with little power over whether or how they were going to be able to provide care alongside their paid work.

We turn next to how these women survived financially in precarious work. The uncertainty of contracts and the irregular timing and low levels of pay created a set of financial coping strategies that are grouped under the theme of 'making ends meet'. Interviewees sometimes found themselves paying up front to work, as temporary contracts were paid at the end of a period of months and nursery costs and transport all had to be settled before their pay came in. They often ran out of money towards the end of a weekly or monthly pay period, having to refrain from spending on essential items such as food or school uniforms, and even having to sell items, take payday loans or resort to informal borrowing from family. Transport costs and the costs of sending remittances to family abroad were factored into their budgets, leaving less for them to live on.

All of this provides important context for understanding these women's working lives and their ability to balance precarious work with care. The lack of choice in work combined with the lack of ability to negotiate pay, low levels of pay and the fluctuating nature of pay all constrained these women's overall bargaining power when they took on precarious jobs. With these constraints in mind, it made sense that interviewees were often very focused on obtaining future work and securing more regular pay. Later chapters turn to the question of how the women felt about the idea of negotiating for care-friendly hours or even disclosing a care obligation at work. All of this was shaped by the pressure they were under to provide an income for themselves and their families.

Starting precarious work

Overall, interviewees reported having immediate financial reasons to take on precarious work, for example being "in a crunch". They were also very astute about the types of jobs that would be available in the local area, noting, for example, when the local job market offered mainly very low hours positions in retail. When necessary, these women took on multiple jobs, often of different types, to increase their income or advance their qualifications. In the following account, women's experiences are grouped by type of contract because this was important to their 'bargaining power' in the workplace, as we will see in Chapter Seven. Understanding the different reasons why the women took on specific types of contract – for example zero-hours contracts – helps us to develop a more rounded picture of the constraints they later experienced when trying to balance precarious work with care.

Zero-hours and agency workers

According to the Women's Budget Group, 54 per cent of those in the UK on zero-hours contracts are women.[1] Women working on zero-hours and agency contracts interviewed for this study included retail workers in high-street chains, higher education workers and care workers. A common theme was that workers did not feel they had a choice about taking zero-hours work.[2] Sometimes this was because the need for immediate work was pressing, and there was little time to wait for the right job to come long. Sometimes these workers concluded after a long period of trying to get a better-protected job that

---

[1]   Women's Budget Group (2020) *Women, Employment, and Earnings: A pre-budget briefing from the UK Women's Budget Group.* Available at: https://wbg.org.uk/wp-content/uploads/2020/02/final-employment-2020.pdf

[2]   This resonates with the findings of a TUC-commissioned survey of zero-hours workers. When asked why they had taken zero-hours work, the most commonly given reason was that it was the only type of work available. See further TUC (2017) *Great Jobs with Guaranteed Hours: What do workers really think about 'flexible' zero-hours contracts?* Available at: https://www.tuc.org.uk/sites/default/files/great-jobs-with-guaranteed-hours_0.pdf

they would have to take precarious work instead. For example, Renuka had a degree in biomedical sciences and spent some time looking for jobs that would draw on her knowledge. But when she was unsuccessful, she applied for all the jobs she saw were available, and she was offered a zero-hours retail position in a high-street stationery chain to cover the Christmas period. She very quickly found that she would be called in "at the last minute" and this would clash with childcare. At the time of interview, she was still applying for jobs in the biomedical sciences field but also hoped to gain a permanent position in the store. In turn, Nuala said that she took a zero-hours job as a cleaner because she did not feel "adequate enough" or "clever enough" to apply for a better job that used her degree.

Another theme was that workers took zero-hours work thinking that they might be able to fit it together with their care responsibilities. Indeed, Nuala took the cleaning job because she hoped it would be easier to fit around care. Chapters Three and Four explore the intense work that the women then put into providing and arranging care around precarious jobs which were, for the most part, inflexible, and the problems they encountered when they needed to disclose a care obligation at work. Yet making decisions about how to work around school holidays and other care-related rhythms often required some sacrifice, and to this extent, the shape and routine of care obligations did shape women's decisions to take precarious work. Bettina spoke about the "flexibility" of her zero-hours role in an elderly care job, which she chose so that she could take time away to care for her daughter during school holidays. But doing so also meant she took a financial hit, due to lack of paid holiday entitlement:

'It's a very flexible contract. In a way, I need it because I need to look after my daughter in the holidays and things … The drawback is that, as I say, if I don't work I don't get paid which is pretty dire during six weeks holiday'.

And in at least one case, it was necessary to move to zero-hours work when flexibility was not forthcoming in other roles. Chantelle was a qualified nurse whose partner often had to travel abroad. Her request for flexible working in a care home where she had a permanent job was turned down on the basis that no one would agree to fill in for her and that she would be at risk from being reported to the Nursing and Midwifery Council if she left her post during a shift. As a result, she gave up that position and took on agency care work in order to manage working alongside caring for her two children and studying for a higher degree:

> 'I was pushed into agency work because it was more flexible with my studying and children. You know how sometimes at work, you start from eight to eight, it's twelve-hour shifts. I had asked if there was anything I can do in terms of picking up my children from school. They said no-one would be willing to come and cover my shift from five to eight. They also said: "You will have to answer to NMC", that's the nursing and midwifery council. Because if you leave the work, you have neglected your patients'.

To this extent, care did affect women's decisions to take zero-hours jobs, but in the examples where this was the case, their care arrangements were fairly rigid, involving school routines and holidays that needed to be covered. In other words, zero-hours jobs were not the flexible response to care that they have been presented to be. Indeed, there was some scepticism of zero-hours contracts. Melanie, a higher education worker, even went as far as saying that she had turned down a zero-hours contract, and that as a result, she was probably going to be unemployed.

Workers on temporary contracts

Women constitute 54 per cent of temporary workers, and increases in temporary and involuntary part-time work since

2011 have been borne disproportionately by women.[3] Women on temporary contracts interviewed for this study included care workers, a short-term seasonal retail worker and workers in higher education involved in research, teaching, web design and careers advice. Their contracts ranged between a few months (the shortest of which was three months) and five years. Some of these workers held multiple contracts of different types, one or more of which could be a temporary contract and the others either zero hours or part time. The reasons these women gave for taking on temporary contracts reflected those given by zero-hours workers: they needed the work for financial reasons, including transitioning off benefits or being "in the crunch". For example, Melanie, a university lecturer, took a short-term and low-paid teaching contract for reasons of immediate financial necessity, but also viewed a temporary contract as a potential "foot in the door" for a career in higher education. She talked about not understanding very well what contract she was signing:

> 'I looked at the hours and the pay and I was like that is extremely disappointing, but right now, I'm in the crunch, I have nothing else, I'll take it and we'll see where we go from there. It's a foot in the door. I didn't know very well what kind of contract I was signing, at all'.

For most temporary workers, the hope was to gain future contracts, longer contracts or a permanent position, even if on a fractional or part-time basis. For example, Donna undertook short-term teaching work at a university for the summer and then found herself able to teach at short notice when needed. She did well and then was able to take on more courses when her employer was in need of a teacher at the last minute. She hoped to develop her career in higher education, but at

---

[3]   Women's Budget Group (2020). See fn 1, this chapter.

the time of interview was still employed on multiple short-term contracts.

A permanent contract, to these women, would feel like they were "moving forward", as Tina put it, referring to her own transition away from a temporary contract and onto a low-hours fractional contract:

'Even the fractional contract, which is very small, you know, one fifth of the contract, was enough for me to feel like I was moving forward at least a little bit. It wasn't ideal. It wasn't actually enough in any kind of large existential sense, but it was enough for me to concretely move some more forward'.

Another reason to advocate for permanent contracts was that they could protect workers who otherwise felt at risk from 'silent' redundancy processes in large institutions, where non-renewal of the fixed-term workforce was used as a way of cutting staff numbers in advance of a formal redundancy procedure.

Workers on low-hours permanent contracts

Workers on low-hours permanent contracts were included in the study because of links between part-time work, low pay and precarious living conditions. The Women's Budget Group has termed these contracts 'involuntary part-time' contracts and notes that 57 per cent of such workers are women.[4] These contracts were included in the study because they were offered without the alternative of full-time employment and provided very low hours with associated low rates of total income. Interviewees in this category were for the most part employed in the retail sector, in chain department stores and

---

[4]   Ibid. See fn 1, this chapter.

supermarkets. They also included academic staff who held 'fractional' contracts (fractions of a full-time equivalent role). The working hours of the low-hours permanent workers ranged from five to 16.5 per week.

The reasons women gave for doing this work included: their having been given the role to replace an hourly paid position as part of processes of workforce regularization in higher education; the lack of availability of other types of work; and working tax credits requirements. A particular theme was that short-hours permanent contracts were the only type of work available in an area or with a specific employer. Sandy worked for a supermarket in a town in Wales and spoke about the lack of other jobs:

'I know that there is nothing about. Not here, not in this area. I would have to travel to Newport or Cardiff and then it's back to the childcare issue … Retail are the only jobs and they are all part-time positions. The only full-time positions now are the managers. It's better business sense to hand out eight-hour contracts or twelve-hour contracts. They are no good to anybody'.

Similarly, Kelly worked for a department store in Liverpool, and said she wanted more hours. She said no other jobs were available that offered more hours and fitted with working tax credits requirements:

'That was the only job I could get. They were all 16 hours. Nobody was offering more. I would have liked to have done more. Obviously, not too much, because how it works with tax credits is very strange'.

Interviewees were critical of the saturation of their local labour markets with very-short-hours contracts with few other options, some speaking unprompted about the difficulties of not being able to get more hours, and the potential legal effects of these contracts. Zoe, who was out of work at the time of interview, said she had noticed supermarkets offering employment, again in Liverpool, for only eight, 11 or 12 hours per week. She had come to the conclusion that these positions would not suit her because she would not be able to negotiate more hours if needed. She felt they were targeted at women and structured so as to avoid employment rights:

> 'What you'd have to do would be to probably to work for two employers. But then you'd probably not be protected then, because of the amount of hours that you are working. I came to the conclusion that a way of employers getting around affording employees certain rights was to keep their hours under a certain amount'.

Multiple contracts

Women took on additional jobs when they encountered problems in their current job relating to pay and conditions, care arrangements or career advancement. For example, Bettina held what she called a "proper job" working as a warden for a sheltered housing scheme, and she also held a zero-hours job working as a sitter to relieve carers. While she enjoyed the sitter job, and found it easier to manage alongside caring for her daughter, it was the warden job that provided sick pay and holiday pay. Yvonne was a part-time cleaner who tried unsuccessfully to obtain training that her employer offered to others through the training options available in the big business that employed her. When she had trouble accessing this training, she took on another job as a cookery teacher on short-term contracts for an organization that provided classes for young people, gaining catering qualifications along the way.

By contrast, Nuala held two separate contracts associated with the same employer for teaching in a prison. She had been offered one job that would encompass the two roles, but had worked out that it would result in a lower income overall, so she decided to keep the two different contracts:

> 'My problem, at the moment is if I take a fractionalized contract full time, I will actually lose money. At the moment, I do seven sessions anyway, annualized, and then the other two sessions I get paid for. So I get paid at the same rate as the annualized contract, which is £22 odd an hour. But I wouldn't be able to do that then, I'm just expected to do the classes and not get paid extra for it'.

As a result, Nuala had decided to keep going with the two separate contracts for the time being because it was more beneficial to her. Finally, Tina spoke about other people in her workplace taking multiple jobs because their paid hours of work on their fractional contracts were too low for them to make ends meet. However, she said this would be too tiring given her care commitments and that she would be too stressed. So instead, she asked her employer to either increase her fraction or consider her for a voluntary severance scheme.

Structural discrimination

Structural discrimination describes a situation in which an organization's policies or general way of working discriminates against people on the ground of their sex, gender, race, disability, age, sex or sexual orientation, or the intersection of these grounds. It can happen at the level of government policies (for example, around economic policy) or at the level of the labour market or individual employers. This kind of discrimination has significant financial, emotional and practical effects on people. It also creates the conditions in which harassment and other types of more obvious in-person discrimination can flourish. Indeed, the difficulties that women face balancing care with work, described in this book, are essentially structural; they come from the way in which government responds to the task of providing unpaid care for others, and the way that employers structure their workplaces and contracts. Yet the women interviewed for this study gave other accounts in which particular types of structural discrimination affected their ability to find work and/or continue in work. For example, Esmat had fled Iran and was now living in the United Kingdom. She had a catering qualification and tried to obtain a job in London, but described being shut out of employment because the jobs in restaurants were reserved for British people first, and then Indian or Pakistani people after that. At one point, a potential employer suggested she might find it easier to get work if she removed her headscarf. As a result of failing to find work in catering, she moved to the North East and took on a zero-hours job with a cleaning company, and then a live-in job as a carer. At the time of interview, she was unemployed again. In this way, experiences of taking multiple short-term or precarious jobs were also associated with structural racism in the labour market.

Surviving in precarious work

We have just seen that the women interviewed took on precarious work largely because they needed a job and these jobs were the only ones available to them in their sector or geographical area. Other themes included the fact that women were in an immediate financial "crunch", that they had been trying to get other types of work but had been unsuccessful and that they needed a second job to augment their income.

Once they had started work, interviewees faced a range of immediate and longer-term financial challenges. The available work was low paid and even below minimum wage. Pay was unstable and fluctuated week on week or month on month. Interviewees spoke of having little left over at the end of their pay period. They adopted a number of strategies to cope with this, including intense budgeting on groceries, selling items, going without new clothes or shoes for their children and paying attention to providing food. Remittances, transport costs to and from work and nurseries or schools, and the costs of borrowing all added to their regular expenses. Interviewees also faced problems with housing, including unsuitable or overcrowded living conditions or difficulties obtaining a mortgage.

Pay

None of the women interviewed on the project reported negotiating their pay. Employers set the pay level and the women felt they had to accept it. As Jane, a temporary worker, put it: "Usually they suggest how much I'm going to get paid". A prevalent theme was that the pay was unsteady, sometimes fluctuating weekly or monthly depending on the employer's needs and the shifts they offered. This was especially the case for zero-hours workers or workers on short temporary contracts. Catherine worked in further education and talked about managerial decisions impacting on her pay through "variable" hours. She said that she only got hours if her employer needed her, and that the employer would cut the hours "if somebody else comes in or it changes or they don't need to fund a class anymore". Managerial decisions about shift allocation could result in women's hours changing on a weekly or monthly basis. For example, Renuka's hours fluctuated week by week in her retail job. She said that she had 30 hours the week of the interview, she would have 40 hours the next week, and that two months prior to the interview she had been getting 20–25 hours a week. Bettina worked as a sitter for elderly people on a zero-hours basis and her pay was entirely dependent on her clients' needs. She talked about her pay "fluctuating":

'It fluctuates so much, because she might, I work like for somebody for a year and then he died unfortunately, then you've got wait until you get somebody else. But I'm going to be quite busy shortly, because I've a lady

Monday that I'll be doing four hours. Tuesday, I do four hours ... Wednesday I usually do five hours. But I've only just found out the lady I look after Wednesday afternoon has got breast cancer as well now, so I don't know'.

Indeed, care work could come to an abrupt end and this could have significant financial effects. Esmat got a job looking after an elderly woman with dementia for three days a week, round the clock, on what she understood was a permanent basis. This paid about £600 per month. As a result of getting the job, Esmat stopped claiming housing benefit. She did not have much left over at the end of the month but was paying her own bills. After about a month, the woman's health deteriorated and she went into hospital. The women's daughter told Esmat that she was no longer needed. Esmat had only worked for eight weeks.

Low pay

Another prevalent theme was low pay, sometimes below minimum wage levels. Most of the interviews took place in 2015 or 2016, when the minimum wage levels were £6.70/hour (for ages 21 and over) and £7.20 (ages 25 and over) respectively. On this study, women from a Bangladeshi background had very low pay, and this resonates with the findings of other studies which show that the ethnicity pay gap for Bangladeshi women is particularly big.[5] Jobs in care and cleaning provide

---

[5]   According to Breach, A. and Li, Y. (2017) 'Gender Pay Gap by Ethnicity', London: Fawcett Society, the pay gap between White British men and Bangladeshi women is 26.2 per cent. See further: https://www. fawcettsociety.org.uk/Handlers/Download.ashx?IDMF=f31d6adc-9e0e-4bfe-a3df-3e85605ee4a9. See also Office for National Statistics (2018) *Ethnicity Pay Gaps in Great Britain: 2018*, which reports that in 2018 Bangladeshi employees earned on average 20.2 per cent less than White British employees. See further: https://www.ons.gov.uk/employmentandlabourmarket/peopleinwork/earningsandworkinghours/articles/ethnicitypaygapsingreatbritain/2018

extremely low pay, especially when they are done on an informal basis. For example, Sada had a part-time job picking up two children from school and staying with them until their parents got home. She worked five days a week and was paid £100 per month. Amina earned on average £10 per hour for cleaning. The highest she had been paid recently was £30 per hour and the lowest was £2.50 per hour.

Hidden low pay

Low pay could be hidden by employer practices, including how the pay was calculated. In Nuala's cleaning job, she was given a certain number of rooms to do in a particular shift, and if she went over she was working unpaid. Often the hotel would host stag nights, so the cleaning would take much longer. Women working in zero-hours or temporary positions in further and higher education reported that the contracted hours they were given anticipated a range of extra activities – for example preparation work and student meetings – that were unpaid. This could be confusing. Donna worked as a temporary lecturer in a university and said that the complex calculations about what would be included and what would be excluded from the hourly rate of pay increased her sense of the pay being unstable, because she felt like she was getting tips for the work, not being paid in a usual way to do it. Catherine and Melanie both said that they had calculated that the work they put into preparing their teaching in further and higher education, respectively, put them under the minimum wage.

Another theme of the interviews was that the number of hours the women were contracted to work was simply too low to support them and their families. Tina had a permanent position on a 0.13 fraction of a full-time job in a university, which paid £500 per month. She said this kind of job could not provide her with a "decent wage". This theme was reflected in the interviews given by women working on low-hours permanent contracts in retail, for example in supermarkets.

One such worker, Sandy, said that she did not want to go back on benefits, but she felt that she was working for "virtually next to nothing" with no spare income, and she had not had a holiday in years. As she put it: "I think, I work so hard to be this poor". Similarly, Sally, a supermarket worker on a permanent low-hours contract, said it felt like everything was "month to month":

'It does feel like everything is just month to month and just making it through the four weeks. Pay day, you're always really excited for that one day and the day after you are just like okay, back to waiting, back to budgeting and everything'.

It was not always the case, however, that women felt their precarious work was low paid. Chantelle had left her job as a nurse in a care home when she was refused a flexible working arrangement. In her new job as an agency worker, she said she was earning double what she used to earn and had been able to buy furniture, take her children on holiday and had more money overall to spend.

Paying to work

Interviewees on temporary contracts reported that due to late payment of their wages, they could find themselves effectively "paying to work" due to upfront transport and childcare costs. Donna said she would be paid at the end of her teaching contract but in the meantime had spent over £350 in travel costs and had paid for her son's nursery. She managed this by transferring money out of a savings account. Jane, a university researcher, often found herself paid very late or having to chase her wages. She started one job in February and did not get any pay until the end of July due to problems with human resources setting up her employee account.

In this way, women's diverse experiences of low pay and late pay affected their ability to budget on a regular basis. Interviewees reported not having much money left at the end of a week or month. For example, Kelly earned £300 per week in her retail job but paid £200 per week to a nursery and also had to pay travel to and from the nursery, her other daughter's school and her own work, as well as pay for groceries. As a result of similar pressures, women reported a range of strategies for making ends meet.

Making ends meet

Women reported trying to ensure that bills were paid first, although Sandy, a supermarket worker, said that when she had been very short on money and had the choice whether to buy food for her children or pay council tax, she had paid for the food. Careful budgeting was also widely reported, with women paying attention to where groceries were cheap and changing their shopping accordingly. However, budgeting was difficult for Sally because she had dyslexia. She found it tricky to work out when the bills were coming out and how this would affect the amount of money she had left to spend. At times, she had to take items back to the shop because she realized she could not afford them.

Other strategies or practices that women reported for making ends meet included using savings, borrowing money set aside for children and selling items on eBay, Gumtree or at car boot sales to make money. Women reported simply trying to spend as little as possible. Zoe was unemployed at the time of interview but had recently worked in a seasonal retail job. She said that her children had worn the same shoes to school for two years in a row, and that each of her children had only two shirts, which she would wash through the week. Zoe said that she had become "very very thrifty". Interviewees paid particular attention to their ability to provide food for themselves, their children and loved ones. When Esmat lost her care job and her income, she was able to go to the local mosque, which was serving free food during Ramadan. Kelly would make a big pan of "scouse", a meat stew local to Liverpool, which she would use for multiple meals and also freeze. For Chantelle, it was very important to be able to put food on the table for her children, because when she was a child and her mother worked away from home, there were episodes when she and her siblings had only one meal a day. This was one of the reasons why Chantelle accepted as many zero-hours shifts as possible. Zoe said that she bought very little in the way of food, with the result that she and her children were "probably underweight".

Another cause of anxiety was the cost of transport to and from work or between jobs. Bettina said that she did not get paid for travelling between her care jobs, some of which were as far apart as Leeds and Wakefield. This had a significant effect on her budget. Fiona worried about how to pay for petrol to get to work and back alongside housing costs, groceries and paying off her debts.

Some of the women also factored into their budgets the need to send money to relatives abroad through remittances. For example, Sada worked as a child minder on an income of £100 per month and sent money to her three children in Bangladesh. Zainab worked as a dressmaker and sent money to her relatives in Bangladesh; her children were with her in the UK. And Amina worked in catering and cleaning on an average wage of £10 per hour. She sent money to Bangladesh for her seven children, as well as saving money in order to pay for them to move to the UK in the future. The expected costs of immigration for family members led women to budget very carefully and make financial plans well into the future, over many years.

Finally, borrowing was a widespread theme in the women's accounts. This included using credit cards for regular expenses such as transport costs and bills. For example, Bettina used a credit card for petrol when she was low on money in her account. As she put it: "I've got to work and I've got to have my car". Tina said that she and her husband would run up debt on the credit card when they were short on money, and then pay it off when he had work. Renuka said that she had used payday loans to help pay for school uniforms, children's shoes, groceries and car repairs. She said this was less embarrassing than borrowing from friends but that she was not always able to pay the loans back on time because she did not have the money. Sharon was a care worker and had experienced periods of time unemployed. She was paying off an "individual voluntary agreement" which the Citizens Advice Bureau had helped her to arrange. She was also paying off debts associated with council tax and TV license bills.

Housing

Housing was a cause of anxiety for the women interviewed doing precarious work, for reasons relating to unsteady work, difficulties paying rent or a mortgage or difficulties obtaining a mortgage. Interviewees reported living in housing that was unsuitable or too small for their families, or sharing with friends or relatives. We have already seen that Esmat lost her care job when her client was taken into hospital. She had just found a flat to rent and been made to pay £800 for two months up front, which she understood as being because she was a migrant and did not have a guarantor. She also paid £200 for agents' fees. She had to borrow from a friend to pay all of this, and when she later lost her job, she lost her flat and moved in with her friend. Zoe had just moved into a smaller rented house with her two sons after a long period of dispute over the mortgage on the property she had shared with her ex-partner, who was abusive. Tina was living in a housing association flat in central London, with a park nearby that she and her children enjoyed. However, the flat was very small and had only two bedrooms. She and her husband had "stacked" their three children up in one bedroom and fantasized about buying a caravan to travel out of the city on holiday.

For those who could consider getting a mortgage, precarious work presented further challenges. Temporary and zero-hours work made it difficult to prove a regular income for a mortgage lender. Dipika was in her fifties, had recently split with her husband and had custody of their two children. When she was turned down for a mortgage on the basis of her temporary job, she emailed her line manager to explain the effects of her temporary status on her housing situation, because she wanted them to understand the implications of that kind of contract. Catherine, a teacher in further education, found it very difficult to get a mortgage because she and her husband were both in their fifties and did not have permanent employment. She said that it had been difficult to produce evidence of regular income.

Conclusion

This chapter has shown that the women interviewed took precarious work because they needed to provide for themselves and their families financially and there were no better options that they could see at the time. These decisions, often made quickly and in situations of pressure, had ongoing effects on their lives. Starting in a job that was not already shaped to meet their care needs meant that women had to either absorb the stress of unsuitable work schedules themselves, through carefully constructed daily routines and care networks, as we will see in Chapters Three and Four, or take the risk of raising a care problem at work. Chapter Five covers the many reasons why raising a care obligation in a precarious job was very difficult for the interviewees, and Chapters Six and Seven go on to explore what happened when the women's care obligations inevitably came up at work, how employers responded and what the women did next.

In the meantime, once they started work, the women struggled with low levels of pay and incomes that fluctuated considerably, leaving them with dilemmas about how to make ends meet. As we have seen, the women took on strategies such as budgeting carefully, selling items and refraining from spending even on necessary items. They paid attention to food and remittances. Due to insufficient pay or unexpected expenses, they took on borrowing through credit cards and payday loans to pay for clothes, bills, transport costs and car repairs. All of these issues of pay and finances had a bearing on the pressure the women faced and provide further context as to why they often felt as if they could not talk about their care obligations at work, as we will see later in the book. In situations of low pay and unsteady incomes, it was very important for the women to secure further shifts and stay in work. Simply put, their ability to risk making a request for care-friendly work was much lower than it would have been had they been in 'standard' jobs. Yet, as the next chapter shows, the daily routines of providing care for others shaped the women's lives to a great extent.

Key points

- Women did not have a choice about taking precarious work. They took zero-hours, temporary or low-hours jobs because they needed the money and because there was a lack of other work available to them in their sector or geographical area.
- Employers set the rate of pay and determined the shift rotas or working patterns.
- There was evidence of structural racism in women's access to work and in women's pay rates.
- Women's pay was unstable and fluctuated week on week or month on month. Women reported low pay and pay below minimum wage levels.
- Women coped with fluctuating pay through strategies aimed at making ends meet, such as going without basic necessities, selling items and using borrowing to cover bills or emergency spending. Fluctuating pay affected women's housing options, causing difficulties with rent and mortgages.

- Bangladeshi women experienced very low pay.
- When women started their new job, they had very little power to negotiate care-friendly work patterns. This meant that they began work in their new job having to absorb the stress of balancing precarious work with care.

THREE

Providing Care: Daily Routines and Experiences

Care drove these women's need to get work and shaped their ability to perform particular types of job. It structured the women's lives on a financial, relational and emotional level. For these reasons, this book focuses on women's experiences providing care *before* it goes on to cover women's experiences at work. This chapter describes the types of care these women performed, who they cared for and how, their daily routines and how they scheduled care. It concludes by exploring the emotional and wider effects of care on women's lives: the feelings they reported in trying to balance care alongside precarious work, and their sense of being overwhelmed and exhausted. Chapter Four goes on to describe and explore care networks: the varied webs of family, friends, nurseries, partners and ex-partners, grandparents, schools and care workers that women weaved together in order to provide care around their precarious jobs.

Interviewees provided unpaid care in a range of ways and through multiple care commitments. A common theme was women performing what Carers UK has called 'sandwich care': caring for a dependent under 18 years of age while also caring for an adult.[1] Care was needed in specific daily and

---

[1] See further Carers UK (2012) 'Sandwich Caring: Combining childcare with caring for older or disabled relatives'. Available at: https://www.carersuk.org/for-professionals/policy/policy-library/sandwich-caring

weekly rhythms, fitting around other care providers, hospitals and schools. Women's daily routines involved getting up early, engaging in sequential periods of care and work with little "wiggle room", sometimes going without sleep, and providing care in their own homes for adults or making regular visits to other people's homes. They scheduled care around work, sometimes finding out late about last-minute shifts, and using strategies such as phoning around, diarizing and using shared calendars to coordinate care around their jobs. Unpaid care therefore involved significant emotional, intellectual and physical effort. Women reported feeling out of control, pulled in several directions, anxious, distracted, sometimes depressed and often overwhelmed. This was the context in which they turned up to work, managing uncertain shift patterns on zero-hours contracts and performing short hours or temporary contracts.

Types of care

Care is notoriously difficult to define, involving a wide range of activities, relationships and emotional work inside and outside of the home that is oriented to another person's daily and/or developmental needs.[2] Some of these activities are obvious: toileting and hygiene; discipline and socialization of young people; feeding and attention to nutrition; organizing care provision with external care providers such as nurseries, care assistants, homes and schools; monitoring or administering medication; education; attention to emotional and social well-being and physical safety; and enjoying the company of the cared-for person. Other activities are much more specific and

---

[2] For a detailed analysis of how care is provided, resourced and governed in the UK, see Elias, J., Pearson, R., Phipps, B., Rai, S.M., Smethers, S. and Tepe-Belfrage, D. (2016) *Towards a New Deal for Care and Carers*, London: Political Studies Association Commission on Care. Available at: http://www.commissiononcare.org/wp-content/uploads/2016/10/Web-Care-Comission-Towards-a-new-deal-for-care-and-carers-v1.0.pdf

connected to the relationship between the person providing and the person 'receiving' care. For example, providing care for an adult relative with a mental health problem might involve helping them to secure housing through liaising with mental health services and a housing association, as well as more daily routines of keeping in touch.

The women who gave interviews for this study had six broad types of caring obligation, which often overlapped. These were: care for a child without disabilities; care for a child with a disability; care for an adult with a disability (for example a parent or partner); care for 'wider' family including grandchildren, aunts or self-defined family members; care for multiple people including across generations; and care obligations abroad for children or adults. These types of care required distinct skills and strategies. For example, women with school-aged children reported concerns about their educational attainment and tried to help with homework where possible. Women caring for parents with dementia or Alzheimer's helped with washing, dressing and feeding, and often had to involve care workers.

Additionally, women's care responsibilities showed a broad definition of family, encompassing a range of people who employers did not always recognize as appropriate recipients of care (see Chapter Six). Interviewees reported having care obligations for adult brothers and sisters, aunts and uncles, parents-in-law, grandchildren and other people who had played important roles in their own or their partner's lives. As such, the definition of the type of family connection that would lead to a care obligation was context specific, but those with obligations falling outside of Western, nuclear family norms could face problems with employers. Tara, a supermarket worker, put it this way:

'You've got to understand that we live in a society now where it's not just mum and dad and kids. You've got step families. You've got extended families. You've got mixed families. All sorts. Actually, my dad was brought up by an aunt, not by my grandmother. So you've got, you know, kids being brought up by different relatives that they classify as their parent. You need to make allowances'.

As we have already seen, multiple care responsibilities were common, with women managing simultaneous care for young children and elderly parents, for example, or for an adult child with a disability and a parent with Alzheimer's. And care obligations changed over time, such that a woman might gradually take on more care for an elderly parent, for example, or relinquish aspects of that care to paid care assistants.

Nuala was a teacher on a variety of different contracts, including zero hours, and the single parent of a son with an autism spectrum condition. At the time of interview, her father was dying and she was managing care for her son around hospital visiting hours with the help of her mother.

Sada lived with her mother, who was frail and forgetful, and she worked as a part-time child-minder. Sada was a single parent for three teenage children who lived in Bangladesh. She had recently applied to bring the children to the UK. She sent much of her wages home to help pay for the children's needs, including the costs of education.

Sharon was out of work at the time of interview but had recently worked on a zero-hours contract as a care assistant. Her adult daughter had a severe disability, resulting in limited mobility, fitting, round the clock care needs, and multiple specialist appointments. She provided care for her daughter with the help of her adult son, who claimed carer's allowance.

Daily routines

Exploring routines and scheduling is important for understanding how the women interviewed for this book managed to provide unpaid care alongside precarious work. Interviewees generally gave accounts of very full days, comprising both paid work and unpaid care, often starting early, with multiple phases and little "wiggle room". They used a range of scheduling techniques to manage care either on their own or within care networks across working days or weeks. Some examples of daily routines are quoted here at length in order to give a sense of how the women described their activities.

Carol, a part-time supermarket worker, cared for her mother-in-law who had Alzheimer's:

'I was getting up at half past four on a morning and I was sorting myself out. Getting myself ready for work and then going down. I'd get to hers about half past five, quarter to six. I'd start doing her breakfast and then I'd go in and get her up and then she'd have her breakfast. And then I would get her in shower and get her out of the shower and dress her and then that was it, I was having to come to work. I was getting home about half past five, six o'clock. I was in bed for half past seven. I had no life. No life whatsoever'.

Chantelle cared for three school-aged children around her night shift agency work:

'I do a night shift. Come home and get the boys ready. When I drop them off in school, I come home and I have just an hour or so to get ready and then I will go uni. And then, by that time, it's around 12 or thereabouts. I come back home and I get a bit of sleep. I make sure I don't go to bed, because if I go to bed, I will sleep and not wake up. I just stay in the recliner really and doze off. And then I will go and pick them up and they finish at three. Usually, when I am dosing on and off maybe I've got chicken in the oven. By the time I bring them home, I just know that I am going to just boil some rice or something for them to eat. That is it really. I can feed them and go to my bed'.

At the time of interview, Nuala's dad was seriously ill in hospital and she was coordinating visits to him around care for her school-aged son, who had an autism spectrum diagnosis:

'I set off from my house at quarter to seven in the morning. I get home from work at about half past six. I go straight out to my dad to see him and spend until about nine o'clock with him. When my son comes home from school my mum feeds him. I'm still at the prison [her workplace] or with my dad. Saturdays I work. The reason I do that is so that I can pay for my son's tuition as well, extra tuition. And then I come home. If I get the chance I go to sleep for a couple of hours just to have a rest or I go to my dad's. And then Sunday is a day of washing, ironing, shopping and lesson planning for the week to get through to the next weekend'.

Getting up early

A common experience reported by interviewees was having to get up very early in order to do care-related activities before starting work. Such activities included getting children up and feeding them and taking them to nursery, or dropping children with family. Where the care was for an adult, morning routines could involve leaving the house and travelling to the house of the cared-for person. For example, Carol, the part-time supermarket worker quoted previously, described getting up at 4.30 am in order to get her mother-in-law showered and give her breakfast before starting her own supermarket shift at 8 am. Another example is Linda, who worked in customer services. Her mother had dementia. Linda would get up at

5.30 am to make her mother breakfast and give her medication before going to work.

Little "wiggle room" between activities

Interviewees described days that were filled with sequential care and paid work activities, which left no "wiggle room", were often rushed and gave women very little "down time". Even though Linda spent over an hour in the morning with her mother before her own early shift, she felt like she had not given her enough time:

> 'I start work at eight o'clock, so I would get up at half past five to get to my mum's for six. And then, I would make her a brew and do her some breakfast. Give her any medication that she needed. And then I'd leave then about ten past seven. So, I used to feel like I didn't give my mum the time she needed, really, because by the time I got there, did what I did, I was going out again'.

Fiona, a supermarket worker, slept at her mum's house before her shifts, and got up at 5 am to start work at 6 am. Her mother would take Fiona's daughter to nursery. Once Fiona finished work, she picked up her daughter from nursery and then had sole care of her until bedtime. Often Fiona then went to bed at 8 pm, leaving her no time on her own. As she put it:

> 'I never ever get a break. I literally leave work, pick [daughter] up, play with [daughter] and feed her, entertain her until she goes to bed. I don't get a chance to have a little nap. I am absolutely exhausted'.

Sam cared for her husband, who had suffered a severe stroke. Her daily routine involved care workers coming in three times and day to feed and change him. During the rest of the time,

Sam and her daughter shared responsibility for feeding him, giving him medication and doing the washing. Sam would arrive home from work in the evening, attach her husband's feed, and then sit down to have dinner at about 7.30–8 pm, after which she would do cleaning and washing.

Going without sleep

A further theme was the women's often having to work through the night, either on night shifts, like Chantelle, or in order to combine work and care with studying. Janice, for example, had a job organizing Ann Summers parties alongside studying for a degree as a mature student:

> 'I would go to university during the day. I would come home and feed my kids and then I'd go out and do a party. And then doing my assignments until about five o'clock in the morning'.

Interviewees also talked about going without sleep in order to manage care, work and other regular commitments, whether this involved getting up early to provide care before work or coming home from a night shift and doing care and cooking during the day instead of sleeping. Given that the interviews only measured one snapshot in time in the women's lives, it is possible that care-related lack of sleep recurs throughout their lives; for example, happening while they are raising children and then again when caring for an elderly parent in their home.

Transport

Transport was an important element of the women's daily routines, whether transporting children to and from school or nursery or travelling themselves to one or multiple jobs during the day. Interviewees described spending a lot of time on transport, making multiple journeys per day for work and care reasons, some of them planned and some of them unplanned. These journeys affected their ability to establish a manageable rhythm of work and care. As we have seen, Sharon shared care for her adult daughter in her home with her son and worked herself as a carer on what she described as a zero-hours contract. For a period, Sharon was working 30–60 hours per week, from 7 am to 9 pm, and travelling to appointments in her car over considerable distances in Liverpool. Sam worked for a supermarket petrol station and commuted to and from work on the bus for 60–90 minutes each way, while also caring for her husband at home. When she sketched her experience of work and care, she drew a bus with the caption "Stressed and depressed" (Figure 3.1).

Tara talked about how she managed travelling to and from her parents' house, 12 miles away, as well as taking them to medical appointments. Getting her parents to the hospital on time required forward planning and leaving her home well in advance. Tara often did multiple back-to-back trips in a day:

> '[When] they've got a hospital appointment, I have to leave home before seven to avoid the traffic to get to their house and then make sure that they get to their appointments on time. Some days are hilarious. It's like, "Okay, mum, let's take you", and so I take my mum and I drop her off at the clinic, and then I take my dad to another hospital and drop him off. I go back to pick my mum up, take her home. Then I've got to go back to my dad and sort him out and then bring him home. By the time they both get home they are knackered.[3] (Laughs). So am I'.

Moving between residences

Interviewees reported providing care in adults' own homes that involved visiting daily, sleeping over or even moving in.

---

[3] Knackered: exhausted; tired.

Figure 3.1: Sam's sketch of her bus journeys to work and back: "Stressed and depressed"

Carol went over to her mother-in-law's house very early every morning to help her get showered and dressed and to give her breakfast, before she and her husband eventually decided to draw on the assistance of care workers. At the time of interview, Carol would still visit three times a week around work to knit together and watch television. Tara shared the care of her elderly parents with her sister on a weekly rota, cleaning and cooking for them, taking them to hospital appointments and keeping them company.

Interviewees would also have adult relatives to stay in their own homes if needed. A particular trigger was the illness of adult family members in older age. For example, when Linda's father was diagnosed with cancer it became obvious that he could not move around the house well. Linda decided to move in with her parents to help provide care for her father. After her father died, Linda stayed with her mother in the house for a short period of time and then moved back to her own house and went to see her mother every morning and evening. As her mother became ill with dementia, Linda began going over more often and staying over. She did this for about a year until her mother moved into a home. When Sherene's mother was diagnosed with breast cancer, Sherene invited her to come and live with her. Even after her mother eventually moved out to live with Sherene's brother, Sherene would have her mother to stay with her while she was going through radiotherapy. Sherene said, "It's Asian family" and described how she would look after her grandmother when her children were small.

Younger women reported moving between residences to provide care, taking their own children with them. Both Zoe and Termeh were single parents. When Zoe's mother died, she took her two school-aged sons with her to live with her father, who had Alzheimer's. Termeh spent several years living with her grandfather who had Alzheimer's. She provided full-time care, scheduling with others in order to be able to even leave the house, feeding him, washing him, looking after his finances and liaising with nurses. At the same time, Termeh cared for her young son.

Scheduling

Scheduling care around work took a lot of effort and ingenuity. Interviewees talked in detail about the process of arranging care when they were notified of their shifts: scheduling school drop-offs and pick-ups with their partner, for example, or phoning around their relatives to share care between them. Sally, a retail worker on a permanent low-hours contract, said arranging care in this way for her young son could be "a bit gruelling" and take between five minutes and a few days, depending on her relatives' availability. This is covered in more detail in Chapter Four.

The women's scheduling strategies depended on when they were notified of upcoming shifts. When they were notified at the last minute, it was difficult to schedule care and avoid unnecessary transport or other costs. Renuka was on a zero-hours contract and said she was normally not notified of her shifts for the week until Friday of the week before. At that point she would arrange with her husband who would drop off and pick up the children from school and nursery. She would also cook food for the week ahead. Sometimes she would be asked in the morning to come in for an afternoon shift, or she would be asked during a shift to stay later. As Renuka was on a low income, she worried about any unplanned public transport costs for getting into work. More than that, same-day schedule changes created immediate problems for arranging after-school childcare for her two young children.

Donna's shifts were different every week, which meant her plans had to change weekly as well. She had a two-hour commute each way to work, involving train fares that were expensive unless they were booked in advance, and as her son was too young to get himself to and from school, she needed to think about pre- and after-school clubs.

'It's taking forever to plan this. I am always thinking maybe I am buying the train and the club will not be open yet, so what am I going to do with him? It's like recheck and check all the options on the trains, and I have to consider the price of the tickets as well, because they will vary, depending on how close to the date it is'.

The cost of transport has already been covered in Chapter Two, but it is worth highlighting that avoiding expensive peak fares intensified the women's need to plan travel and care exactly. In the context of managing changeable work shifts and care responsibilities, keeping transport costs down led some women to spend a lot of time planning, which added to their existing stress levels.

In addition to phoning around, making last minute adjustments and planning travel, interviewees also reported paying a lot of attention to diarizing their commitments and using calendars collaboratively when necessary. More than one respondent took out her diary during the interview to demonstrate how important it was. For example, Sandy showed me a small paper diary that she said she took everywhere with her. She said that she knew her schedule six weeks in advance to make sure she was not in the situation where "something out of the blue might come up". In turn, Tara talked about the weekly and longer-term work of planning she had to do with her sister in sharing care for their elderly parents. They had come up with an arrangement whereby Tara would work Monday to Wednesday and then care for their parents Thursday to Saturday. Her sister would cover the other weekdays and they would share Sundays. Tara's sister would take care of housework and cleaning, and Tara would make sure that her parents got to medical appointments. This arrangement was fairly new and they were still seeing whether it would work. It involved liaising together about their parents' appointments and other needs. They had a calendar on the wall in each of their homes dedicated only to their parents' schedule. When they called each other with updates, they would then pencil in the arrangements. Tara said that they used wall calendars so that other family members understood what was going on.

What women felt about care

The research underpinning this book understands emotions as signposts to wider social pressures, not just as features of women's individual personalities. My approach has been to observe where emotions and feelings have emerged in interviews and what they have been connected with. When women talked about their emotions, much of what they said concerned the pressures of caring for others alongside work. Some feelings were about the power of work to shape or interrupt care, others were about the effect of care on women's wider experiences and relationships. Women experienced exhaustion and a feeling of being overwhelmed at the inevitable tensions that came with managing precarious work and care. They also felt guilt, shame and resentment. They talked about "not having a life", missing friends and turning into "machines" or "robots". Again, this tells a very different story to the idea of women 'choosing' these jobs in order to balance work and care.

Mothers and role models

The interviewees expressed different feelings about their identities as mothers, and their work ethic helped shape these differences. One theme was about women acting as role models for their children. Talking about the stress of doing zero-hours work, her very low income and her unpredictable shifts, Renuka said that showing that she was trying was an important lesson for her children in "not relying on other people's money": "It is a good example for my kids to see that, you know, mummy is working and not relying on other people's money. Mummy is working. Yes, we're struggling, but she's doing her best".

Another agency worker, Chantelle, talked about the "suffering" and "responsibility" that went with having children. She said it had been her decision to have children and so she should be able take care of them and her husband. She was trying to show her children through her studying that you have to use your hands and use your brains and not collect "benefits and donations or charity".

Another theme was about the difficulty of being a "career woman" and a mother, and the losses involved in choosing work. Nuala, a prison teacher and single parent, was the first person in her family to go to university. She studied for her A Levels and degree after low-paid jobs working as a cleaner. Nuala said she never wanted kids but had her two children because that was what was expected at the time. She had since felt like a "bad mum" and that she couldn't be the mother she wanted to be. She missed out on bringing up her children because she was balancing studying, working and care, and her own mother did a great deal of the childcare as a result. She talked about the idea of being able to have children and go to work, as a woman, as a "fallacy", and that being "your best at your job" would lead to letting your family down.

Worrying while at work

Interviewees reported worrying about their loved ones during their time at work. This led to considerable effort expended maintaining the appearance of what they thought were appropriate emotions in the workplace, when otherwise they were feeling anxious and distracted. Linda was a customer service worker and cared for her mother, who had dementia, before her mother eventually went into a home. Linda worried about her mother using the stairlift when she was not there, and she also worried that being distracted about her mother might lead to performance issues and eventual disciplinary action.

> 'Sometimes I would find myself sat there thinking, I wonder what me mum's doing now and I hope she's all right. She ended up staying upstairs all the time before she was actually went in the home. I was sad about that. She had a stairlift and I thought, I hope she doesn't try and get off'.

Linda spent a lot of time worrying about whether to give up work, but found this circular, as she also then worried about not being able to afford this and also not being able to get extended leave to care for her mother.

Tina worked in a supermarket and was aware of the impact of care-related anxieties on her, and her colleagues', ability to maintain a cheerful impression with customers. This was particularly important because 'mystery shoppers' would provide regular feedback on whether employees had been welcoming. Tina's mother had to have several operations at short notice, and her sister called Tina at work to update her about it. Her manager said to her, "There's always something wrong with your mum", and Tina felt that she had to put on a brave face and carry on working.

Guilt

Women reported feeling guilty about not being able to do more for the people they cared for due to their jobs. Jane had a young daughter and worked on temporary contracts as a university researcher. She said she felt guilty not being there for her daughter when she had to work, and she also felt guilty about finding out that she didn't have any work to do and had wasted her mother's time asking her to provide childcare because nursery was too expensive and inflexible. She said her husband did not feel the same level of guilt. Donna said that with all the commuting to work and teaching preparation she needed to do, she was not able to give her children the time she thought they needed. She said that she felt that society was putting her under pressure to work and not spend as much time with her children.

Women also reported feeling guilty about their loved ones going into care homes or about not being able to do more for them when they were in care homes. Linda talked about the guilt associated with helping her mother move into a care home when it became too difficult to look after her in her own home:

> 'There was a lot of guilt. There is guilt all the time, really, when you are caring for someone and you want to … I've had a good family. I've had good parents and you want to do the best for them. I would never have wanted to have let them down in any way at all. I still feel guilty now, sometimes, when I go to the home to see my mum'.

Being pulled away from children by work

When the women felt their work and the social conditions around their work were preventing them from spending more time with their children, then as well as feeling guilty they also reported feeling resentful or sad. Catherine described her son coming to visit her in her home office when she was doing teaching preparation. She would try to have him near her with his toys. But she also felt resentful that she was put in the position of working when she could have been spending time with him. Sada was very upset to be far away from her children, who lived in Bangladesh. She lived with her mother and cared for her, as she was forgetful, alongside doing a child-minding job and sending money home for her children's school fees.

Witnessing decline

Women who cared for elderly relatives talked about the feelings associated with witnessing their progressively worsening health. This brought feelings of sadness and loss, but also a specific sense that there were a set of identifiable stages of decline, which they could see happening with their own elderly relatives, and which might create intensified care burdens in the near future. Catherine got on very well with her mother, who was living in a care home and whose physical health was declining. She talked about the difficulty of seeing her "go downhill":

> 'My mother was my rock. She brought me up. She was there for me all the time. She never remarried. She never had any other relationships or anything like that. And to see her actually, she's 90 now, going downhill very quickly, physically, luckily her mind is still intact. It's difficult, it's hard'.

Linda said that she could identify the stages that her friend was going through with her mother-in-law, and she knew what the next stage would be. Bettina's mother had dementia and was still living in her own home at the time of interview. Bettina talked about having a "feeling of impending doom", because she was well aware of the stages associated with the progression of dementia. Her mother could still do many things for herself but Bettina said she knew things would get worse and her mother would no longer be able to cook for herself and there would be a risk of her wandering. She could see that in the near future she would have to be a full-time carer for her mother, but in the meantime she only needed to do her mother's cleaning and would just keep "battling on".

Effects of work and care on social life

We have already seen that the women described very busy daily routines with little "wiggle room" between work and care. This left little time for socializing. For example, Sam said that following her husband's stroke she had lost her independence, because it was no longer possible to go out for a meal, a drink or a show with a friend. She said everything had to be planned. Linda talked about how she stopped doing yoga and going on holidays and to social activities when her mother started getting ill. Carol said that she had "no life": she had no time to socialize or to rest properly, and got to the point of being burnt out before she and her husband made the decision to draw on the help of care workers. When they did this, and Carol cut her hours, she said she felt like she was "getting the old me back again".

Friends were very important, but finding time to see them alongside precarious work and care was difficult and sometimes impossible. For example, Chantelle said she did not have time for a social life, and that even if she did go out, she would be thinking of how much she could be earning as a zero-hours worker instead. She said that going out would have to be worth more than what she could earn. She spoke about losing friends because she was too busy to stay in touch:

'I have lost a lot of friends. At the moment I don't have anybody because even when people phone me I'm too busy to talk to them. So the only people in my life are my children, my husband, my supervisors at the university and my agency that I work for'.

On the other hand, Catherine talked about regularly calling friends when she had experienced problems at work. Whereas her husband would "bottle up" difficulties with caring for their elderly relatives, Catherine would speak to friends going through similar issues, and she found this very helpful.

Feeling overwhelmed

Interviewees talked about how managing their jobs alongside caring for others left them feeling exhausted and overwhelmed. Their daily routines could feel relentless, and they craved time to themselves. Women talked about feeling robotic, like a "machine" or a "headless chicken", or as if they were on a "hamster wheel", as the following interview excerpts show. This indicates that these women had a sense that they had lost some control over their own lives. A connected theme was their feeling pulled apart by competing responsibilities: "Torn in all directions", as Catherine put it. While women described coping, or "carrying on", their descriptions of their schedules and routines show how much emotional work and logistical effort was required to provide care for others alongside precarious work. Excerpts from the women's interviews are given here in order to convey their feelings in their own words.

'I'm knackered. I'm absolutely exhausted. But like I say, I'm a machine. I don't mean that in that, in a big-headed way. I just mean that it's just the way I were brought up. You just carry on'. (Nuala)

'I suppose it's like being a robot on automatic pilot. You get up, you get showered, you get dressed and make sure [husband] is all right. Give him his medicine and that. My daughter comes by and I say, Bye, I am going to work.

Go to the bus stop and get on the bus and go to work and do your job and then the cycle is reversed. You are just like a robot'. (Sam)

'If I really sat down and thought about it, it feels like it's just, you are just kind of holding on every month. Month to month, with everything: with money, with work, with you know, sanity, you feel like you are just getting through each month'. (Sally)

'I am just barely hanging on. I feel as if, if I didn't have the children, I'd be more than happy to be hospitalized. I would really love that. I would love to just be in hospital and just be tranquillized. But the children have only got me. They would come under the care of social services, wouldn't they, if I wasn't there'. (Zoe)

'Right now, I feel like I am, you know, I am running like a headless chicken. It would be good to have some order in my life back again and a regular income coming in, so I know what money is coming in'. (Renuka)

'I never ever get a break. I literally leave work, pick [daughter] up, have to play with [daughter] and feed her, entertain her until she goes to bed. I don't get chance to have a little nap. I am absolutely exhausted'. (Fiona)

'You need time to just, like, be and not just like this relentless hamster wheel'. (Tina)

Conclusion

This chapter has explored the care responsibilities interviewees had alongside their precarious work. These women often had multiple, shifting care responsibilities, which had significant effects on their daily lives. Daily and weekly routines involved providing care themselves either in their own homes or in other people's homes (or both), liaising with care providers, taking adults to hospital appointments, cooking, cleaning, preparing food and helping with dressing and washing for children and adults, as well as providing entertainment. The stress of providing and arranging care alongside uncertain, intermittent or irregular work resulted in these women feeling overwhelmed and out of control. These feelings, and the experiences and social structures that led to them, are important, because they helped to shape the women's approach to disclosing care to managers or colleagues or even asking for flexibility at work. In other words, these feelings were shaped by the contracts women were on and they also, in turn, had legal effects. They impaired the women's ability to negotiate better conditions either immediately or in the medium term to help them balance work and care, as we will see in Chapters Four, Five and Six.

Key points

- Before assessing why women in precarious work found it so hard to manage, it is important to understand the nature of the unpaid care they were providing.
- Care structured women's lives on a financial and emotional level, and often drove their need to get a job. This unpaid care was complex, time intensive and logistically challenging.
- Interviewees provided a wide range of unpaid care for others, including care for their own children, relatives, family members or loved ones. Women commonly had multiple care responsibilities at the same time, for example for children and elderly relatives.
- Women's daily routines involved getting up early, little "wiggle room" between activities, going without sleep, concerns about transport, and moving between residences.

- Women put a lot of effort into scheduling care around work and planning travel by using diaries and calendars.
- Women reported feeling overwhelmed by the pressure of providing unpaid care alongside precarious work. They felt responsible as role models for their children. They worried about loved ones while at work and felt sad or resentful at time taken away from being with them. They witnessed the decline of adult relatives. They had less time for socializing, and lost friends as a result. And they talked about feeling like a "headless chicken", a "robot" or a "machine".
- Emotions like this were not only shaped by the kind of precarious jobs the women held, but in turn affected what women felt they could do to address any problems at work.

FOUR

Care Networks

As we have seen from Chapter Three, interviewees provided much care themselves through very busy daily routines and rounds of scheduling around their precarious work. However, as this chapter shows, women also played the role of care coordinators. This meant that the women felt ultimately responsible for organizing care and helping with large decisions; for example, deciding whether an elderly relative should move into a home, or helping a parent with mental health problems to liaise with service providers. Essentially, women organized other family members, co-parents, schools, nurseries and paid care workers to provide care in what this study terms 'care networks'.

I have dedicated a chapter to care networks because they were so important in the interviewed women's lives. Care networks describe complex, collective and multi-institution arrangements involving different forms of informal and formal care provided by family, friends, schools, nurseries and care workers. Care networks might be fragile or partial, leaving women with much of the day-to-day work of providing care, or they might provide valuable, regular wrap-around support.

Women interviewed for this book reported that their care networks allowed them to access precarious work in the first place – the networks were shaped in such a way that they fitted around the irregular, episodic or interrupted work schedules the women had. When care networks worked well, they were invisible to employers. When women arrived at work, the employer would only see one person, not the rounds of telephone calls with family or ex-partners or quickly made bargains with friends. If the work pattern was changed or cancelled, as often happened in precarious jobs, an entire network of people was affected. At the intersection of care networks and precarious jobs, these women provided a crucial buffer zone, resolving tensions, coming up with solutions and allowing each employer to imagine that the worker was available to them without other obligations.

Creating and maintaining care networks around precarious jobs required these women to develop distinct scheduling skills and practices and led to time-intensive consultation with groups of people and care providers. This chapter begins by describing what women did when care networks involved friends and family members. It then moves on to describe how women incorporated schools, nurseries or other paid care providers into their care networks. And it concludes by reflecting on how care networks, and women's associated care strategies, help us appreciate the intensity of work and care pressure that these women were under in their precarious jobs.

People involved in care networks

Interviewees reported coordinating networks of varying sizes involving their partners and/or ex-partners, adult children, parents or parents-in-law and siblings. Many respondents were single parents and coordinated with adult children, ex partners and others to provide care. Each type of relationship brought its own experiences and challenges when it came to organizing care alongside work.

Single parents

Single parents reported feeling that it was difficult to cope because they performed the greater share of care and had ultimate responsibility for making sure care was covered, even when ex-partners were nearby and relations were amicable. Single parents used a wide range of strategies to provide care for their children and for the other adults for whom they assumed care responsibilities. Fiona said that things were "quite tough" and that her decision to sleep over at her mother's house to manage an early shift alongside caring for her daughter was due to her ex-partner not providing enough care. Dipika talked about feeling responsible for many aspects of childcare, including a large mortgage on a house that was well situated for the children's schools. She said that while her ex-husband lived close by, she provided "nine tenths" of the care for their two teenage children. Because she often had to travel for her job, she worried about leaving her children on their own and had interviewed a student for the job of staying overnight with them while she was away.

Voicing difficulties common to other single parents on the study, Sandy referred to the challenge of paying all the bills on her own on a part-time wage while trying also to arrange care around her shifts. In particular, she talked about the difficulties of finding childcare to cover early mornings and evenings:

'Most of us want to set a good example for our children. We want to work. But we need full-time positions and we need some sort of childcare solutions for the early mornings and the later evenings, because not everybody has got somebody that can have the kids'.

Being solely responsible for childcare had other knock-on effects. For example, Kelly, a low-hours retail worker, described paying a large amount of money on local transport costs because she had to drop one daughter to school and another daughter to nursery, and these were both some distance from her work in the city centre. Finally, single parents reported paying particular attention to providing out-of-school activities (for example, Boys' Brigade) and educational stability for their children.

Partners or ex-partners

Again, interviewees reported a range of agreements with partners or ex-partners concerning care. Sandy worked at the weekends, when her ex-partner could take the children. When the children were ill, she would take time off unpaid to be with them. Women who worked fewer or more intermittent hours than their partners talked about negotiating over who would take time off work when children were ill. Catherine was a teaching assistant with previous experience as a fixed-term worker in further education. She would sometimes ask her husband to take a day off work or work from home when she needed to go into work unexpectedly; she called this "juggling". However, she experienced friction in the relationship when she needed to work in the evenings and spent less time with him and their child as a result.

Adult children

Adult children were involved in durable care networks, as we will see later in the chapter. For example, Sharon and Sam each relied on their adult children to help provide care for disabled adults in long-term arrangements. In other cases, adult children could assume care responsibilities. Linda was a customer service worker. Her mother had been diagnosed with dementia about two years prior. Linda said she felt she had the support of her three adult children and that when she couldn't take time off work, they could step in. Similarly, Tara said that when she or her sister could not provide care for her frail parents, her sons would take over.

Parents

Workers had mixed feelings about involving their own parents in care for their children. Some felt it would not be fair. For example, Sandy's mother had died and her father had a disability. She said that even if her parents were fit and able to do it, she did not think that it would be fair to involve them because there should be other arrangements possible. Other interviewees had recently relied on their parents for help with care but now found their parents were too infirm. Bettina's mother had helped with the care of her two sons, who had now left home. However, as she had just been diagnosed with dementia, she could not now help with the care of Bettina's daughter. Instead, Bettina was providing care for her mother.

In other situations, grandparents were healthy and willing to help with care, which could involve a considerable commitment. Yvonne's mother had moved in to provide care for Yvonne's two school-aged children while Yvonne worked two jobs as a cleaner and a cookery teacher. Yvonne could not otherwise afford childcare. Fiona was a single mother with a low-hours, part-time job in a supermarket. She did not get much help with care from her toddler's father, and as she had to get up at 5 am to get to her shift (which started at 6 am), she stayed three nights per week at her mother's house. As we have seen, Fiona's mother would take her daughter to nursery.

Grandparents also provided care in interviewees' homes. For example, Simone had three children under 18 and one child of 19. She was studying for a university degree alongside preparing to take up a job as a care worker through an agency. Her mother picked up the children from school and stayed with them until Simone finished studying at about 8 pm. Jane was a temporary researcher in a university. Her daughter had recently started nursery, but previous to that, Jane's mother would come over to the house and care for her while Jane was working.

Siblings

Sisters and brothers helped with care in a variety of ways. For example, Tara (a supermarket worker) shared care of her frail parents on a weekly basis with her sister. They had each arranged their work so as to provide daily care and be able to drive their parents to hospital and doctors' appointments. Catherine was a teaching assistant. She and her sister shared visits to their mother, who was in a care home nearby. Sally worked in a betting shop and was able to ask her brother to take care of her eight-year-old son when needed.

Friends

Friends were felt to be important, but the women's experiences of being able to keep up with friends, or even rely on them to help with care, varied significantly. A common theme was regret at not having the time to keep up with significant friendships due to balancing work and care. Sandy, a supermarket worker, said that she would not expect any of her friends to 'pop round' because they all worked. On the other hand, Tina, a fractional worker in higher education living in London, talked about informal networks of friends and acquaintances helping her to cope with not having family nearby.

Family or friends not nearby

Not having family or friends nearby could be due to bereavement or relocation, and it meant women did not have the range of possibilities for establishing care networks and managing work around care that other people, including their colleagues and managers, would expect. Sandy put it this way:

> 'I really haven't got anybody, as such. People don't seem to realize that my mother passed away nearly twenty years ago and it is just my father and my brother; my father's just not well enough. Those that know me well, they know my situation, but sometimes when you speak to managers they find it a bit unbelievable, like you are lying'.

Donna had relocated with her husband and family to the UK from Brazil, leaving behind a large network of support. She wanted to compensate for her children's loss of time with their grandparents and cousins, and for the distance from their culture, by spending more time with them herself. Finally, as already mentioned, Tina shared the care of her three young children with her partner. Both had been brought up abroad and their family was mostly overseas. They had saved up to pay for her family members to fly over and take care of the children when they both had work, but it had been very difficult to manage the expense. She talked about establishing a network of support among friends and neighbours in the immigrant population in her local area:

> 'There's all these unplanned things that happen. For that you need a network. Most of the people round here who live in social housing are from immigrant backgrounds, so you tend not to have a big extended family around you. So, you need each other in order to make it work'.

Tina found her local park an important meeting point for socializing and finding care options for her children, finding child minders through word of mouth and "watching" each others' children.

Strategies in care networks

When care networks involved friends, family and significant others, a range of informal strategies emerged, from passing responsibilities between people and "stepping in" to medium or long-term arrangements whereby finances and roles were shared between adults. Focusing on the care strategies as well as the people and care providers involved allows us to build up a picture of what women had to do to manage unpaid care alongside paid work. Even if care networks involved similar people (for example partners or parents) they would result in very different benefits for and pressures on women coordinating the care alongside precarious jobs.

A common strategy for interviewees was passing care responsibilities between other people to fit around nursey or school times, as well as people's work schedules. Women called this "pass the parcel" or "tag team":

'His grandma is really good. She helps me quite a lot. His dad as well, because we share parental responsibility. Worse comes to worst, I've got a brother and some friends who help out as well. As a family we generally have a rule of we all help when it comes to the needs of the children. I'm lucky in that sense … it's a little bit like pass the parcel'. (Sally, retail worker)

'Between me and my husband, we've just kind of tag-teamed with the childcare, because we don't earn enough to pay for childcare'. (Tina, university lecturer)

Interviewees also described loose networks, where another adult would "step in" as required. Sandy was a single parent of two school-aged children. She worked part time in a supermarket and shared care for the children with her ex-partner, who would take the children at weekends. Sometimes Sandy found it difficult to cover periods between her shifts and the beginning or end of school, and at those times, her brother could step in:

'I've been fortunate so far, because my brother has always been on an afternoon shift, which means that he can come in the morning at six o'clock just as I am leaving for work and he can stay here until he starts work at two o'clock in the afternoon. And then I am home by about half past four, so there's only a short period of time where they are on their own'.

As the quotes in this section suggest, care networks varied in size and in the level of regular commitment or planning needed. They might involve a wider range of family members helping out as needed, or two people transferring care between themselves. Care networks could also be relatively longstanding, involving durable arrangements about how a group of adults would arrange their lives to provide care. These arrangements would have implications for a worker's daily routines and finances, with decisions made collectively about who would claim carer's allowance, for example. Sam's husband had experienced a stroke, which meant he needed significant help in the home, with care assistants coming in three times daily. Sam had discussed his care needs with her adult children, and her daughter had taken on care for Sam's husband when Sam was at work, with help from her siblings. Sam's daughter claimed carer's allowance for doing so. Sam worried about her daughter's ability to spend "quality time" with her own children as a result. Another example is Sharon, whose daughter had a severe disability requiring daily care. For around twenty years, Sharon had been managing this care with the help of her son, who now claimed carer's allowance. At the time of interview, Sharon's son would sleep during the day when Sharon was at home, and he would then take the "night shift".

Durable arrangements, however, also changed with the shifting capacities of the adults involved. Bettina's own mother used to help care for her sons when they were young but at the time of interview had been diagnosed with dementia and needed a sitter herself. Bettina said she felt like she had fewer and fewer people to support her now because they were getting older and poorly and needed care. As she put it, "We just stumble through it really".

Another important type of much longer term care arrangement was made by women when they left children in another country to work in the UK. In these cases, women left their children in the care of their husbands or other family members. For example, Sada was living in London and working as a childminder. She sent money home for school fees for her three children in Bangladesh. Amina had left her seven children in Bangladesh and last saw her youngest son four years ago, when he was seven years old. She was also sending money home for the care of her children. While this meant that arranging the care of their children around work on a daily basis was less of an immediate consideration, these women reported missing their children, calling them often and worrying about how they were doing.

Where women relied on other people alongside providing care themselves, it was still often the case that those other people had jobs and their own obligations. This meant that scheduling took time and required intense rounds of consultation, negotiation and emotional labour, which are described in Chapter Three. Despite other people's participation in the networks, women reported feeling that they had ultimate responsibility not only for the care itself but for ensuring that it could continue when they or specific others were not present. This was the case even when loved ones resided in care homes, for example, or in situations where women held multiple care obligations. The metaphors women used for sharing care, which evoked games or sports (for example, "pass the parcel"), were also appropriate for describing this level of responsibility – women would be left holding the parcel when the music stopped. This left the women with a decision to make, between taking time away from work or being absent from caring for a period of time. For example, Linda cared for her grandchildren and also had a mother with dementia. As she put it: "If it ever came down to it … I would have had to say, I will just have to take the day off and whatever consequences there are then I'll have to face them when I come back".

Other women talked about worrying about when children could be left at home on their own. Zoe had been concerned about leaving her teenage sons on their own when she went out to work in her seasonal job, because they had been previously picked up by the police for a minor incident, and she wanted to ensure they kept out of trouble. Bettina, a care worker, said that her daughter was too young at 11 to be left at home on her own, but that she was hoping to be able to leave her for short periods of time when she was 12 or 13.

Care networks involving nurseries, schools and adult care providers

This section covers women's experiences of using external care providers – care provision outside the home, family or friendship network. These include nurseries, childcare, schools, care workers for adults and care homes. It is important to remember that the care networks women talked about included elements of family and friend care alongside schools and nurseries.

Nurseries and childcare

Interviewees were concerned with how to pay for nursery care. This was because the cost was very high relative to the women's pay, and also because the timing of paying nursery fees did not match up easily with the women's fluctuating incomes. Kelly found the weekly cost of nursery care at £200 to be very high relative to the wages she earned from her part-time retail position. In turn, Jane was worried that paying for nursery care would not match up with her income. She worked in higher education on a series of fixed-term research contracts. Her concern was about paying a regular direct debit, as was required by the nursery, when her earnings were not regular. As she put it:

'It's about having the money on time so I can pay for it, because nursery would be a monthly direct debit. Whereas it was a big long period of time where I wasn't getting paid, because of payroll issue or somebody not getting their paperwork into the correct place on time … It's just having it, you know, regularly being able to rely on it being there, which is the problem'.

When interviewees found the cost of nursery too high or unmanageable, one way of coping was to leave work and take their child out of nursery. For example, Tina said she felt like she was working to earn the money to put her children in nursery and that it ended up feeling like a "dead end". So she made other arrangements, including paying for her family to come and live with her for a while to help take care of the children when her husband was working. Similarly, Melanie's husband worked full time and she usually took care of their toddler. She used nursery sparingly, when they could afford it, and for specific reasons, when she felt she needed to advance her career.

When women did manage to secure a nursery place for their child, they worried about keeping it. Interviewees reported not being able to vary the hours they put a child into nursery, even when they were not working enough to justify the cost. Jane's contracts could vary significantly, and even when she did have a contract she would often find that she was waiting for others to complete their work before she could do her work. Had she been able to use a nursery on a week-by-week basis and not pay for a whole year, she would have done so, but this was not possible. Instead, Jane relied on her own parents to provide ad hoc care for her daughter to cover her own inter-mittent periods of work. For Kelly, there was no option but to put her youngest child into nursery full time, despite the fact that her permanent short-hours contract often featured blocks of four hours work per day. Kelly's position was difficult because both her nursery and her employer were inflexible. The nursery required her to commit to paying for full-time care, and her employer often allocated her a shift in the middle of the day (12–4 pm) for three days per week, but on different days each week.

A commonly reported concern was the lack of availability of nursery and after-school care on evenings and weekends and during bank holidays. Kelly said that her four-hour shifts were often on evenings and weekends when her children's nursery and school could not provide cover, and at the time of interview she was just about to work a shift on Christmas Eve. Sandy made a similar point, noting that retail jobs involved hours at any time of day, whereas most childminders did not work before 8 am, after 6 pm or at weekends. She suggested that work-based crèches would be very useful.

Finally, women who used nurseries for childcare feared penalties for late pickup. Renuka worked in a zero-hours retail job and her husband worked in a supermarket. Sometimes they were charged when they were unable to pick up their child from nursery on time. Late penalties were also a concern for Kerry, who despite her low income used taxis to help her pick her children up from nursery when public transport was not quick enough to get her to the nursery on time after a shift.

Schools

Women reported putting significant effort into arranging drop-offs and pickups for their school-aged children around their shifting work patterns. Donna was given last-minute work over the summer as a temporary university lecturer. Her daughter was very young at the time, and her husband worked in a different city. Donna and her husband scheduled when each of them would leave for work and return from work respectively so as to be able to look after their daughter. Interviewees also drew on after-school clubs where possible, which provided care in the mornings and evenings around school hours. They were grateful when these arrangements were flexible, allowing women to ask for extra hours due to a new shift for example, as happened in Catherine's case. However, they also reported fearing penalties for late pickups from such clubs or only being allocated fixed hours every term.

School holidays

Women reported leaving jobs or choosing specific jobs in order to cover school holidays. When they could not take paid leave, one strategy was to request unpaid leave. Catherine worked in further education in a prison but could not take time off during school holidays. She left the job for that reason. At the time of interview, she was about to take up a position as a teaching assistant in her son's school in order to have the same holidays as he did. Termeh was unemployed at the time of interview but looking for work as a teaching assistant. She said that being a single parent, it would otherwise be very difficult to cover her son's school holidays. Similarly, Yvonne chose work as a cleaner in a university because she thought that she would not be needed over the summer vacation when students were not present and that she would therefore be able to take care of her two school-aged children. However, when she asked to take that time as unpaid leave, her request was refused. Had childcare options been available for these women on an affordable basis or free of charge to cover school holidays, it is likely that they would not have needed to make these decisions.

Adult care providers

Interviewees reported feeling grateful to have the help of care workers in looking after adult relatives such as partners or elderly parents. The presence of care workers could allow women to undertake work or mark the end of women's own struggles in attempting to provide care around work. Sam described the care workers who came three times a day to care for her husband at home as "brilliant". With the care workers and the help of her daughter, Sam had moved her husband home from hospital after he experienced a severe stroke, and she also managed to work part time in a supermarket. Carol struggled for a long time trying to care for her mother-in-law, who had Alzheimer's, around her job in a supermarket. Carol and her husband had promised his mother that they would not put her in a care home. But the strain of caring for her mother-in-law had Carol getting up at 4.30 am and going to bed at 7.30 pm, without any time for herself.

For Carol, the involvement of carers helped her regain social connections and establish more healthy routines for herself. However, managing care workers also involved effort and did not always work. Linda cared for her mother, who had dementia, with the help of care workers. Similarly to Carol, Linda got up at 5.30 am to go round to her mother's house and get her ready, before Linda herself went to work in her customer service job. Linda tried to involve her aunt, but her aunt could not always go; they tried carers, but her mother did not like them. They lowered the number of carers' sessions from three times daily down to once a day in response to her mother's wishes, and then they dropped the carers altogether. At this point, social services suggested to Linda that her mother should be in a home. Linda said that having professionals make the suggestion of the home helped her make the decision, because she had promised her mother this would never happen.

It was also the case, however, that interviewees found the cost of care workers prohibitive. Tara split the care of her frail elderly parents with her sister in an intensive weekly schedule because they could not afford to pay for care workers. As she put it: "You are constantly half asleep thinking, god forbid, you know, and they won't have a live-in carer. We can't afford to. Really just cannot afford to".

Tara and her sister engaged in complex co-caring, which required each of them to make the decision to work part time, because they could not afford carers. In other words, the inability to afford care workers had extensive effects on their work patterns and their daily lives, as we have already seen in Chapter Three.

Care homes

Having a relative in a care home changed the type of care that women provided, often marking the end of a period of intense stress and effort. However, women still reported going to see their relative regularly, and this also represented a type of ongoing care or connection that had to be managed around work. Linda went to see her mother in her care home three or four times a week and arranged for her mother to have a visitor every day. Catherine saw her mother every week in a care home close to her home town, but worried about how she would fit this in when she started her new job as a teaching assistant.

Care strategies with nurseries, schools and adult care providers

The care provided by nurseries, schools and adult care providers came with its own rules and schedules, which had significant effects on the women's lives. With some notable exceptions, nurseries, schools and adult care providers generally did not provide the kind of flexibility women experienced in their networks with family and friends. Indeed, women reported fearing penalties for picking up children late from nursery or after-school club if a shift ran over. In order to avoid the cost and shame of such penalties, women defaulted to family and friends when there was a last-minute pressure caused by work. For example, Renuka called her husband when she was called in for a shift at short notice and they needed to pick up a child from nursery. However, these kinds of last-minute arrangements were harder for single parents and for parents without family or friends nearby. In this way, the effect of inflexible care arrangements was felt by women differently depending on the availability of the other people in their care networks.

However, interviewees' strategies with nurseries, schools and care-workers had some similarities with those they used with friends and family. As we have seen, in networks with family and friends, women often made decisions about paid work, care responsibilities, care shifts and who was going to take carer's allowance according to relatively durable patterns. When the care was to be provided by nurseries or schools, women also made significant medium- or long-term decisions about work. When nursery care was too expensive or the payment schedule did not fit with earnings from precarious work, women looked for other care options, again defaulting to providing the care themselves and leaving work or drawing on networks of family and friends. A different kind of strategy was simply paying for much more nursery care than was needed in order to be able to work when required on short-hours job. Additionally, the lack of available cover for school holidays in certain jobs led to some women leaving their work or choosing specific types of job that would fit with educational rhythms, such as teaching assistant or cleaner in a university. All of these decisions had deep and long-lasting financial effects.

Care networks were almost always made up of mixtures of family and friends, nurseries, schools and adult care providers. In this way, women's overall strategies often spanned the different types this chapter has covered. It was not always the case that women would default to friends and family (with associated strategies of "passing the parcel" or "stepping in") if a work schedule shifted. Sometimes this was not possible for personal reasons, including those people's own work schedules or a wish not to trouble them, and women resolved problems in other ways, for example by taking a penalty for late pickup or declining a shift. So while care networks were often diverse, they were fragile: some parts of care networks were more rigid than others, and women had to constantly work to resolve these issues alongside being available for paid work.

Conclusion

Care networks supported interviewees in performing their precarious jobs alongside unpaid care for others. These networks responded to the intermittent or last-minute shifts, evening and weekend work patterns, regular short-hours shifts, or successive temporary contracts that employers offered to women. Focusing on care networks helps us to understand the wider impact of precarious work, showing how last-minute shift changes, for example, affected the wider groups of people who helped provide care around work. Care networks help us to understand the wider social and financial pressures these women experienced. Because the rhythm of precarious work was sporadic, episodic and often interrupted, women were under pressure to create and repair care networks alongside doing paid work and providing unpaid care themselves. As we will see in Chapter Five, this pressure was intensified further by the reluctance women felt even to disclose care obligations at work for fear of reprisals.

The reason for detailing all these networks and their associated strategies in the current chapter has been to provide essential context for the following chapters on interviewees' working lives in precarious jobs, where managers held a great deal of power. The key argument here is that women created the care support for loved ones that allowed them to even countenance taking up precarious jobs. Each precarious worker was supported by a carefully woven web of friends, family and care providers. When workers held back from telling their managers about care responsibilities, as we will see in Chapter Five, or used sick leave to cover a care emergency, as we will see in Chapter Six, they were acting with a wider group of people and care providers in mind.

Unpaid care and paid work never exist in isolation from each other. Yet these women were positioned at the intersection of two distinct spheres: a sphere of unpaid care in which they had to coordinate complex care needs and schedules, and the sphere of work, in which employers only offered them the kind of contracts in which the power to award or deny them shifts or future work was in the hands of their managers. While the women in this study created care networks to allow them to do precarious jobs, the following chapters show that employers could continue acting as if they were employing an unencumbered person, unconnected with others, with no care responsibilities.

Key points

- As well as providing care themselves, women played the role of care coordinators, setting up complex collective and multi-institutional care networks.
- Care networks helped women access paid employment in the first place, but these networks also came to be shaped around employers' needs, as women responded to last-minute shift allocations, for example. In this way, the effects of employers' practices extended much further than to just the worker herself.
- Care networks included adult children, parents, siblings and friends. Single parents and women without friends or family nearby experienced particular problems in setting up and maintaining care networks.
- Women's care strategies depended on who was involved in the network.
- With family, friends and significant others, women used strategies such as "pass the parcel" or "tag teaming" between adults, people "stepping in" when required and long-term decision-making about roles and responsibilities that might involve who would claim carer's allowance, for example.
- With some exceptions, nurseries, schools and adult care providers were less flexible than informal care networks. Nurseries required long-term regular payments, which were difficult on fluctuating pay. Women made significant decisions about jobs in order to accommodate or cover school holidays.
- Women provided a crucial buffer zone between work and unpaid care, resolving tensions, coming up with solutions

and making big decisions that would affect their finances or wellbeing.
- Care networks were crucially important to women's lives, yet often were invisible to employers.

FIVE

"Rocking the Boat": Talking about Care in a Precarious Job

We have seen that the women interviewed for this study did not have much choice about taking on precarious work, did not usually negotiate their pay and were responsible for complex individual and collective arrangements to provide care for others. This chapter moves on to the question of whether these women felt able to disclose a care obligation at work, which is an important step in asserting any of the usual family-friendly rights or in coming to a more informal arrangement. Interviewees reported having little power to negotiate flexible working or to challenge employer-led working arrangements that made care difficult. They focused on the problem of continuing in work with the present employer or finding suitable follow-on work, which resulted in their attention being more on "showing willing" than expressing their need for care-friendly work arrangements. Indeed, these women perceived making informal requests for flexibility to be risky because the requests could identify them as a "liability" to the employers or as "unreliable" in situations where they wanted to avoid antagonizing employers in order to be offered future work. As such, "risky requests" put the responsibility of managing care dilemmas on the women themselves and intensified the stress and the stakes of communicating care needs to their employers.

This chapter begins with how interviewees felt about their work overall. Women described enjoying work, which gave them important social contact and a sense of achievement. Yet women described feeling like "second-class citizens" in the workplace, with worse terms and conditions that others on permanent contracts, and struggling to cope with job uncertainty and last-minute shifts. Women were aware that their jobs could be discontinued with little notice and that they were replaceable. They experienced the combination of job uncertainty and second-class status as a reason not to ask for flexibility at work or even to disclose a care responsibility. They were often already overwhelmed by the stresses of managing care alongside work (what is termed in this chapter "care-fog") and this impeded their taking more proactive measures to find out about their rights or protect their positions. The chapter concludes by suggesting that the idea of negotiating flexible work is particularly risky for women in precarious work, who have good reason to fear "rocking the boat" and avoiding appearances of being "unreliable".

How interviewees felt about work

Interviewees reported enjoying their work but often felt like "second-class citizens". They had to cope with the uncertainty of whether they would even be getting shifts in the coming weeks or whether their contracts would be renewed. Alongside this, a common experience was being informed about work schedules only at the last minute. All of these factors impacted on how interviewees felt about communicating with their employers about their care responsibilities and in turn their ability to assert any rights that were available to them.

Interviewees enjoyed their work

Interviewees talked about work giving them a boost to their confidence, as well as being a vital way of providing for themselves and their loved ones. Zoe had been unable to work for a long period of time due to depression following the death of her teenage son, splitting from her husband and losing her home to repossession. When she took a seasonal job, she was aware that it did not use her degree-level skills, but, as she put it, the job helped her feel like things were achievable: "Managing to obtain even just a very small job that was very easy to do, really was a big boost to my confidence. I felt as if things were achievable and that it would be possible for me to build on that and to move forward".

Alia had come to the UK from Bangladesh many years previously and she struggled with her English-language skills. At the time of her interview, she had obtained a cleaning job and said that this gave her a sense of achievement. Esmat was unemployed at the time of her interview, having worked most recently as a live-in carer for an elderly woman, and previously as a cleaner. A qualified caterer, Esmat was extremely worried about her situation as her housing benefit was about to end, and after that she would need to move in with a friend. When asked to draw how she felt about work and care, she drew a picture of a window, with a scene of mountains, sun, river and trees. Esmat said that she felt that "work is like an open window" (Figure 5.1).

Work also gave women valued time and space away from their care responsibilities, and important social contact. Sam described the lack of conversation at home when she was looking after her husband who had suffered a severe stroke. As she put it, "It's interacting with other people that really keeps me going". Katia made a similar point. She had been a carer for her mother for a long period of time, from at least her own teenage years until her mother's death about a year prior to the interview. She said that work was like a "reward" to her because it gave her a sense of escape and it supported her mental wellbeing: "I've always seen my study place, my work place, as a way to just escape from it all. So actually it's been good for my mental health".

Added to the social contact was women's sense that they were making a difference to other people, and that they were good at their jobs. Again, Katia talked positively about excelling in

Figure 5.1: Esmat: "Work is like an open window"

her work as a researcher "despite everything that goes on". Janice, a prison teacher on many different types of contracts, was even more explicit: "I love it, because I feel like I'm doing something. I feel like I'm making a difference".

Bettina worked as a carer providing respite care for other carers. She had a school-aged daughter and cared for her mother who was in the early stages of dementia. Her step-father also had dementia and was in a care home. Because of this personal experience, she identified with the people who benefited from the respite service:

'It's really satisfying. I know how much they need the respite because my stepfather's got dementia and he's in a nursing home. And I know what state my mum's got into. The relief on their faces when you say to someone you can go out for four hours'.

Like other women, Bettina enjoyed the social contact of the work, and particularly valued talking to older people as part of her job.

"Second-class citizens"

However, alongside enjoying their work, women were keenly aware that their roles were different and of lower status than other people's roles. As Katia put it: "It's difficult because as a fixed-term member of staff, you don't have the full citizen-ship of work". Interviewees described feeling like they were "on the outside" or "dogsbodies" within their places of work:

'From a point of view of being part of the college and part of the team, you are always on the outside. I had a proper career before, where I was a professional and everything. So I felt important … Now I just feel like a general dogsbody'. (Catherine, teaching assistant)

Intertwined with feeling "on the outside" was an awareness of being held back, underpaid or underpromoted for their skill or experience level. Dipika, a temporary worker, explained that she had been on the same grade in her university support role since 1999 and that she felt undervalued. She felt the employer got much more from her than she was paid. This was exacerbated, often, by knowing that other colleagues' terms and conditions within the same organization were much better when they were in permanent roles. Mandy had direct experi-ence of covering a maternity-leave position for a permanent colleague and was asked to do the same work once the cover had ended, but for a third of the pay. She talked about feeling like she had to work harder than colleagues in permanent roles, a feeling that was magnified given the differences in their jobs and pay:

> 'I think I work massively in excess of how I am paid and really what I'm contracted to do, whereas some full-time staff work much less ... So, you know, that is why I feel it's unfair ... it's perhaps magnified in the context of their secure well-paid employment and my insecure, very poorly paid employment'.

Coping with job uncertainty

Coupled with the sense of separateness at work was the need for women to cope with uncertainty about their jobs. Finding out late about work – for example the renewal of a temporary contract – made it harder to plan financially, leading to anxiety and considerable stress about making ends meet. Jane talked about having sleepless nights thinking about whether she was going to get ongoing work as a research assistant, and whether the work would come in time for her to pay her bills.

A common theme of the interviews was that the types of non-standard contract these women held within their organizations made them more aware that their jobs could be discontinued or not renewed with relatively little notice or fanfare. This is not just an individual matter: when large numbers or entire sections of the workforce are employed on temporary or zero-hours contracts, significant reorganizations at work can take place rapidly, as Dipika described it, leaving the women mindful of how precarious their own situations were:

> 'There have been lots and lots of contractors who have been going with no notice, basically. They've been thinking they were on a rolling contract. The IT team that we work with, we were told within three days that they were all going. It has felt realistically very precarious, because there was a staffing freeze as well. So, if you

were unfortunate enough that your contract was going to come up at the time that there was a staffing freeze, you wouldn't then be able to apply for internal jobs'.

Last-minute shifts

A different kind of uncertainty came with shift work. Women on zero-hours or temporary contracts often found out about being given hours or further contracts very late, with little time to arrange care or other commitments. The level and type of fluctuation depended on the type of work. For example, workers in retail and social care found that hours could fluctuate week on week:

'It really depends. This week I've got 30 hours. Next week is a bit more, it's 40 hours for the week. In February was less and I think it was like 20, 25, something like that'. (Renuka, zero-hours worker, retail)

'It kind of ebbs and flows, because just as you think, got a week's work and I'm fine, something happens and that's the nature of the job'. (Bettina, care worker)

There were two prominent themes in the women's accounts of the shifts or patterns of work that were offered to them. First, women had little control over what was offered. And second, the shifts were often last minute or short notice, either due to employers' normal working practices or because employers had to cover for other workers being off.

A lack of control was reported by women in care work, higher education and retail work. Sharon, a care worker on a zero-hours contract, stated that because she had not been given a contract by her employer "he can just go like that (snaps fingers) any time". Mandy, a temporary lecturer at a university, said, "You have very little or no input or control" when it came to finding out about her upcoming teaching for the year. Women also reported that they found it hard to argue against the shifts if they were not suitable. Last-minute or short-notice shifts could mean being given a rota for the coming week only days in advance, being given very variable hours week to week, or it could mean women only finding out weeks in advance of a further- or higher-education course that they were needed in. Sally worked in retail on a permanent short-hours contract and was trying to complete her further education while also caring for her young son. Her working pattern varied and she was only given two days' notice of her rota, leaving her scrambling to arrange care:

> 'It was really hard to manage, because one week I'd be working Sunday and Monday, Thursday, Friday and another week I'd be working Monday to Saturday and my rotas would be done a week in advance as well. I'd only find out two days before the next week started what I'd be doing and then I'd have to run round and get all of that childcare in place, which is quite difficult even with an army of family'.

As we have seen in Chapter Three, Renuka worked in retail on a zero-hours contract, and despite being given a rota one week in advance, would often be asked to cover shifts for other workers at the last minute. Sometimes, her manager would call her in the morning to ask her to cover an afternoon shift, and as well as arranging care at the last minute she would have to find the money for an unplanned train or bus fare. This was very difficult as money was tight.

Variable and last-minute shifts had significant effects on the women interviewed for this project. Some women worked for employers who changed the workers' location of work at the last minute, asking them to cover a different location from their usual workplace. Changes in travel plans often led to changes in care arrangements. Sally was told that under her contract she could be deployed to a different shop at the last minute. This led to problems arranging care, as she describes:

'You could be working two miles from your house one day and the next day you are working ten miles away and they still [think] that's acceptable. There was a particular occasion not too long ago – I was in a shop in [location 1], which isn't too far from my house. A member of staff had called in to see [if she could work] at a shop that was in [location 2], which is about ten miles away. I was told I had to go and work in that shop, because they had nobody else. And I kind of resisted and said: "That's too far for me to get home. And I finish too late. I finish at 10 pm and I've got a baby"'. Their response was: "Well that's in your contract, so there's not much we can do about that"'.

On this occasion, the shop to which Sally had been redeployed was over an hour and a half's travel away by public transport, for a three-hour shift at the end of her working day. She said that she felt she had to do the shift because she understood that otherwise the employer could subject her to disciplinary action.

In this way, the pressures women experienced in coping with job uncertainty and last-minute shifts all affected how they felt about negotiating care-friendly work arrangements. If the job was already changeable and difficult to manage around care, it created a disincentive for women to ask for more suitable shift patterns. Women experienced weekly or longer-term uncertainty as managerial control, not as an invitation to ask for more flexibility to help them manage their own lives.

Communicating with employers about care

This section focuses on whether and how women communicated with employers about their care responsibilities. It includes women explicitly asking for flexible work but also the factors surrounding their even disclosing a care responsibility or making decisions to accept unsuitable shift patterns. This concern of this section is therefore wider than the making of formal 'flexible work' requests, a legal language that most of the women did not use. Interviewees' awareness of legal rights to family-friendly work is covered in Chapter Six. Instead, the focus here is on the broader topic of what the women felt they could disclose or discuss with employers, and why.

Interviewees often did not communicate with employers about care needs even when they had good reasons for needing altered shift patterns or other care-friendly types of work. When they did communicate, they used a range of informal and formal methods of communication, from impromptu chats at work, arranged meetings or the requesting of one-off accommodations, to formally disclosing care responsibilities at job interviews. Their requests ranged from time off to deal with emergencies through to standardized working hours to help them manage intensive care needs for a partner with a disability.

Women's attempts (or their reluctance) to communicate with employers about their care responsibilities were intertwined with what was going on at home or with their care obligation and how they felt about their work more broadly. As Chapters Three and Four show, it was often difficult to arrange work and care at the last minute, and women reported feeling greater pressure when last-minute care obligations came up. As Sandy put it: "Especially when it's spur of the moment, last-minute thing, it's so hard to try and sort something out and quick".

We have already seen that women often enjoyed going out to work but also felt like "second-class citizens". When it came to talking to employers around care responsibilities, another powerful theme was that women reported not wanting to "rock the boat" and feared reprisals for trying to negotiate. However, at other times – or sometimes even intertwined with these fears – women reported more confident approaches, including "fighting" with managers and being "cheeky". This section begins with some important themes about women's feelings and associated strategies, because they provide the background for many of the actions that followed them. As in other parts of this book, the women's emotions are important to the analysis not just because they give insight into their individual wellbeing (or lack of it) but also because emotions are shaped by social context and influenced what the women did next. Chapter Six then goes on to describe how employers responded when women did disclose care responsibilities at work.

"Care-fog"

As we have seen in Chapter Three, the intense stress of managing care alongside work led to women feeling exhausted and overwhelmed. Interviewees described feeling like "robots" or "machines", giving the impression of a lack of control over their own lives. They also talked about feeling fragmented, "pulled in all directions" (Figure 5.2) or like "headless chickens", indicating they felt that the pressures they were under actively disorganized them, making them feel less able to cope. In this chapter, the effect of these feelings is termed "care-fog". Care-fog describes a range of feelings associated with having too much going on at the same time as one is providing care for others. Care-fog includes feelings of stress or anxiety but also the feeling of not being able to process what is happening. It is important to recognize that care-fog was not just associated with care but with the interaction of complex care arrangements with often changing, precarious working conditions. As such, the term is under-inclusive. Nevertheless, bearing in mind the effects of care-fog can help us understand why women did not always take action to improve their working conditions. To be more specific, the stress of managing care alongside precarious work undermined women's ability to negotiate better working arrangements.

For example, Tina, a lecturer, had recently been transferred from a zero-hours contract to a permanent low-hours contract. She said that she wanted to work out how to increase her

Figure 5.2: Catherine felt "pulled in all directions"

fraction and thereby her pay and career prospects. However, she was confused as to how her employer had calculated the fraction and had stopped trying to work it out for this year while she cared for her three children, one of whom was a baby. She said: "I just thought, let me just do what I can do this year with having a baby and two other young children". As long as Tina held off questioning how her fraction had been calculated, she could not understand her contract and was not able to find out what it meant for her career development.

Sam, a retail worker, neatly summarized the effects of care-fog on women's ability to negotiate flexible work. Drawing on her personal experience of negotiating around work after her husband had a stroke, she explained that the emotions associated with an intense new care burden could lead to women going along with management instructions that were not in their interests:

> 'When people go in wanting flexibility because something has happened and they now become a carer, they are very emotional. It's a very emotional time. They might say yes to something when it's not what they want or what they need, because that's what the boss says'.

As we have seen in Chapters Three and Four, the existence of care networks and the difficulties of scheduling care (especially for single parents) meant that when women reported negotiating flexibility at work, they were negotiating against the background of a fragile collaboration achieved with effort and often at emotional cost. When women encountered problems at work, they worried about transferring that stress onto their home lives and other people in their care networks. As Yvonne put it:

> 'Most women take the stress from work to home. You understand me? You don't have anybody to go to. If you go to HR, HR is not in support of you. Where is the avenue for you to turn to?'

Additionally, Sam talked about how the pressure of managing inflexibility at work alongside care for her husband was transferred between her and her daughter:

> 'No, it's the family. This is what they don't understand. It's a knock-on effect that it has on me. How it affects me psychologically, mentally. The pressure then [goes] onto my daughter'.

In this way, care-fog had significant effects on women's working conditions and career prospects. It could prevent women from being able to negotiate better working conditions or even challenging unsuitable situations at work. In turn, because the 'fog' was inherently associated with work pressure, women reported transferring the pressures they were facing in their jobs back onto their loved ones and care networks.

Fear of "rocking the boat"

An important theme was fear of rocking the boat and fear of reprisals. Interviewees feared raising a care obligation at work because of the consequences this could have for getting further work with the same employer. This could mean that they did not talk about their care obligations or kept any mention of care to a minimum, opting instead to take unsuitable shifts, which had an impact on their care arrangements. The fears ranged from a suspicion that the employer might opt in the future for a worker who did not have a care responsibility, to more immediate fears about losing their job. Donna worked as a temporary lecturer in a university and had two children, one of whom was in nursery and the other in school. She did talk about her need to make arrangements for her children's care, but she worried that this would lead the employer to seek someone else for the work:

'I do fear that, at some point, they will be, "Oh no, we don't want her anymore because she's always bringing up the children, let's find someone who lives around and who doesn't have children, because this is a recurrent point"'.

Dipika also worked in a university on temporary contracts and was even less likely to talk about her care responsibilities. She talked about not wanting to be seen as unreliable:

'I just think I don't want to be seen to be unreliable, because I need the job … You can't antagonize people too much'.

When women interviewed for this study talked about being worried or reluctant to raise a care obligation, it was over-whelmingly associated with losing their job or not getting further work. The women who talked about such fears were often (but not always) on temporary or zero-hours contracts, which suggests that in situations where women were aware that ongoing work was at the employer's discretion, they made a negative association between raising a care responsibility and the likelihood of getting ongoing work. Their fears were also connected with feeling that the jobs could be easily given to other people; in other words that there were other people who could take the work instead, in a job market that was tilted in the employer's favour. Renuka worked in retail on a zero-hours contract and said that she would not turn down shifts for care-related reasons because she needed the job:

'I need the job … I couldn't possibly not get paid. I have to deal with it … I wouldn't be that brave to go to my employer and be like, right, this is not working'.

Janice had previously worked in a very low paid, zero-hours cleaning job, and while she was often given her shifts at late notice, she felt she had little option but to take them because the employer could give the work to someone else:

'You had to do them hours. You had to commit to a certain amount of hours otherwise you wouldn't have a job, because they'd give it somebody else'.

Similarly, Sally had a permanent, low-hours job in retail and feared asking for flexibility because it could lead to her losing her job:

'They make you feel like if you don't like it, leave. We'll find somebody else and given the current like job market, that's a scary thought, and it's a scary, like, process. To be jobless feels … like, I'd panic'.

Women already went over and above to prove their reliability in order to secure ongoing work. Disclosing a care obligation or asking for flexibility risked the goodwill they had built up, which underpinned their ability to work and provide for their loved ones. For example, Renuka talked about not wanting to negotiate her hours too much because she was holding out for a permanent contract. Chantelle was a registered nurse and worked for an agency on a zero-hours basis. She often did more work than needed so that the care homes would request her from the agency:

'I am grateful they give me the full shifts. I have met people and they will say: "I am not getting any shifts". Whenever I am working, I make sure I do a little bit extra than what the agency is supposed to do … I know I am supposed to go in and give medication in the morning and I have that option of just leaving everybody lying down as long as they are safe. But I would go to the extent of maybe even preparing breakfast … I am trying to do things so they will call me back'.

Women talked about needing the work because they had children or other adults depending on them. This meant that they could not "rock the boat" at work. The need to provide for others financially could mean that women would not ask for flexibility or enforce any rights they knew they had, as Dipika explained:

'I feel my kids depend on me. This is the best option I've got at the moment, because I need to keep them where they are … I've got to keep this job. I can't do anything too much to rock the boat. I mean, I'd be stroppy at work and so on, but I couldn't enforce legal rights'.

The fear of being at risk if they mentioned a care responsibility was accentuated by feeling under added pressure when the employer knew the worker was a care provider, and by feelings of shame associated with trying to balance work and care. Renuka was aware that her employer knew she had children and was constantly worrying that the employer would penalize her if she did not agree to particular shifts:

'You are under pressure with that. Will you still keep your job if you say you are not coming in for one of the jobs? Would they penalize you for being a mother because you have childcare responsibilities? So I feel like I am pressured into going into a job, or they have tested me'.

Dipika spoke about being willing to raise her care responsibilities with her employer, if needed, despite her fears (outlined in the previous quote) about being seen to be unreliable. However, doing so reminded her of negative feelings about being a single mum balancing care with work. She said there was something "grubby and shameful" about it and that it was not possible to make it look easy:

'I am quite willing to say risky things, to make myself vulnerable in a professional context. It's just that there's something quite grubby and shameful about being a single mum with care responsibilities. You can't just make it look easy'.

In this way, interviewees described feeling that they would be causing problems for employers if they refused shifts or asked for flexibility: the onus was on the women themselves. Not only that, but women experienced ongoing background fear about losing their jobs for raising care responsibilities and were mindful of the risks of "rocking the boat". Not being able to "make it look easy" made women uncomfortable in their jobs but also underpinned their concern about losing the ability to provide for others if they were upfront about needing to organize work around care.

A common experience among those who reported feeling like they could not "rock the boat" was having encountered previous difficulties at work trying to negotiate around care or problems with career progression. As we have already seen, Dipika held off on applying for a promotion that she later saw a male colleague gain while she stayed in the same pay grade as she had been in for many years. Chantelle took up working for an agency on a zero-hours contract after she had been refused flexible work in her previous permanent position. Sally experienced multiple instances of inflexibility on the part of her employer when she had been asked to work at different locations at the last minute or when her line manager had been insensitive around her son's care needs when he split his head open at school. This suggests that the fear of rocking the boat was connected with existing employer inflexibility: women sensed a negative environment and made a realistic assessment of their chances of negotiating flexibility in the future.

Feeling confident

Another important theme in the interviews, however, was women describing themselves as confident and giving examples of situations in which they had asserted themselves with their employer. In the interviews, women used phrases such as "having guts", being "proactive", not "bullshitting" and "always fighting" with managers. All of these women were on permanent short-hours contracts. It is possible that women on zero-hours or other types of precarious contracts had also taken such an approach, but they did not report it in interviews.

Some women who described fearing reprisals also described being confident either before or after having problems with balancing work and care. This suggests that the women interviewed for this project were not inherently frightened of any employer but instead experienced fear in particular working situations. The risk of rocking the boat was an aspect of the working relationship itself, which could be managed in certain circumstances. For example, Janice described having to take a certain number of hours in her previous job as a cleaner. However, in her current job as a prison teacher, she felt more able to say what she thought:

'I get into trouble at the prison, because I always say what I think. I'm known for that. I always say what I think, I don't bullshit'.

It is possible that Janice's improved status in her new job gave her more power to assert herself at work. Other women working in educational roles talked about asserting themselves at work alongside being aware of the risks of reprisals. In the previous section, Donna (a temporary university lecturer) described being concerned that people at work would think it would be easier to employ someone who lived locally and who did not have children, because she did raise her care obligation at work when she needed to. However, Donna also described being "cheeky" about asking the finance office to explain her complex pay slip, which was the result not only of different contracts but of a very complicated method for calculating pay:

'I'm kind of cheeky. I will go there and ask, "Can you explain me what this means, how much am I going to get at the end of the month" or get my payslip and say, "What is here?" … I have the guts let's say to go there and ask … "What is it here and can someone break this down?"'

While in an ideal world, it would not be seen as "cheeky" to ask how one's pay is calculated, doing so was a source of pride for Donna and left her feeling like she had "guts" to assert herself if needed at work. Similar approaches were reported by Katia (a temporary university researcher) who talked about being "proactive" about getting help, and Mandy (a temporary lecturer) who made annual requests to be put on a fractional permanent contract:

'I'm quite a proactive person. If I know that I need help, I will go out and I will seek it'. (Katia)

'Every year, I put in a request to be transferred to a fractional contract, because the remuneration policy allows for this, but in practice it never actually happens. So each year I sort of say, I want to be made an FTE employee and every year they say, no'. (Mandy)

When retail workers described being assertive, by contrast, they talked about "fighting". For example, Sam (a supermarket worker) encountered problems at work after her husband had a stroke. She eventually became more confident in her approach toward her employer. Her view was that she was also fighting for others:

'You get to a stage with work where ... enough is enough. I had just had it. You can threaten all the time and I said to her, just don't threaten me. Do it, I said and you will see where it goes ... I am fighting for everybody in the same situation'.

Similarly, when Tara was put through disciplinary action for taking time off to care for her mother-in-law, she described realizing that she needed to fight:

'I suffered from stress, depression, but I thought to myself, I'm not going to give up. I need to fight. And it took five months for the appeal hearing to be heard'.

Feeling confident could therefore indicate a sense of desperation or of having to fight as well as a willingness to take a longer-term proactive approach with an employer. It indicated that women were ready to question or challenge in certain circumstances and that fears of rocking the boat were not down to women being inherently afraid but more about women assessing the situation at work and being realistic about their chances of obtaining better conditions or staying in their jobs.

Conclusion

This chapter has focused on how women felt about their jobs and how they approached formally or informally negotiating around a conflict between work and care. Generally speaking, women valued being able to work, even if their jobs were precarious. It was important to the women interviewed for this project to be able to provide for themselves and their loved ones, and paid work gave them self-esteem and a different focus than that of providing unpaid care. However, an important theme in interviews was that women also felt like "second-class citizens" or "on the outside" in their jobs, and they encountered a high degree of job insecurity. These feelings suggest that women were acutely aware of their lower status within the workplace and accurately sensed that they had impaired bargaining power with employers. Women also often grappled with "care-fog" at times when they could have been trying to assert their needs or obtain better terms and conditions. Where women encountered problems at work with inflexible or hostile managers, they reported feeling less likely to make a request around care in the future. The prevalence of last-minute shift allocation, and a lack of control over shifts, added to the daily sense that women's continued employment was at the discretion of their manager.

These women's lower status, often last-minute schedules and job insecurity combined to create a fear of reprisals and a reluctance to "rock the boat" when it came to disclosing a care obligation to an employer or negotiating care-friendly work. The immediate stress of care itself could also impair women's ability to muster the necessary confidence to negotiate a sensible working arrangement. Women's sense that children or other loved ones depended on them heightened their fear of being seen as unreliable and losing out on continued employment. However, the existence of more confident approaches to employers suggests that women's fears about disclosing care were strongly associated with their status and workplace environment, not just features of their personalities. Where women did manage to maintain a confident approach to their work and their employer, they derived confidence from saying what they thought, asking questions about pay and "asserting themselves" or "fighting" with employers over shift allocations and disciplinary action.

All of this suggests that for women in precarious work, the stakes of disclosing a care obligation, or trying to arrange work around care, are very high. The fear is that by disclosing care, women will lose out on upcoming shifts or even lose their jobs. Being seen as unreliable is dangerous for women in a context where the employer has the discretion to award next week's shifts or renew a temporary contract. It is even more dangerous when women are coping with a care emergency or a shift in care that requires their urgent attention. For these reasons, negotiating flexible work is much more risky for pre-carious workers than it is for 'regular' employees. In the next chapter, we turn to the question of what happens when the women in this study managed to disclose a care responsibility despite such risks.

Key points

- Interviewees reported enjoying work because it provided them with self-confidence, time away from a care obligation and other benefits apart from the pay.
- However, women often felt like "second-class citizens" in the workplace, with little control over job uncertainty or last-minute shift allocations.
- Women experienced the uncertainty of precarious work as being a result of managerial control. This uncer-tainty undermined women's capacity to ask for flexible work arrangements.
- Women reported being cognitively and emotionally overwhelmed with the pressure of providing care alongside

work. This could be termed "care-fog". Care-fog explains why women often did not take action to improve their working conditions.

- Women feared reprisals for disclosing a care obligation at work. They needed to ensure immediate future work and this undermined their ability to negotiate care-friendly working.

- Sometimes women were confident in the workplace, talking about "being proactive" or "fighting with managers". This indicates that women's fear of "rocking the boat" was not an inherent feature of their personality but strongly linked with their working conditions.

- Overall, however, women felt unable to disclose care responsibilities or negotiate care-friendly work patterns for fear of reprisals, losing their job or missing out on future shifts.

SIX

How Employers Responded

'When my husband first had his stroke ... I was a team leader at work. But when he had his stroke and I couldn't work 24/7, I could only work like 9–6 or 8–5 Monday to Friday. They didn't want to support me. I had to step down to a general assistant because they didn't want to help ... They said, in that role, at that time, as a team leader, you had to be flexible and work a rota within the seven days a week [sic], which I couldn't do'. (Sam, supermarket worker)

Chapters Three and Four showed that work and care interrelated in women's lives to a great extent. Care was never absent from these women's working lives, even when it might be invisible to managers and co-workers. Women put immense work into setting up, maintaining and repairing care networks, using personal relationships, scheduling and many other strategies to manage care while they were at work. As such, we could describe the relationship between care and work as being dynamic, with these women at the intersection between the two spheres, trying to manage their precarious employment alongside their unpaid care responsibilities. Chapter Five focused in particular on how women felt about their jobs and what factors encouraged or prevented them from disclosing a care responsibility at work. Due to the power imbalance at work, women often refrained from "rocking the boat" for fear that they would lose out on future work by being seen as "unreliable".

This chapter focuses on what happened when it became inevitable that they disclose a care responsibility to a manager; when women could not smoothly manage the tense juxtaposition of shifts, care responsibilities and wider care networks. In other words, this chapter focuses on the moments when the unpaid care work that women did became visible to managers and co-workers. Sometimes this was due to a change in the care needs of a loved one: a health crisis for example, or a change in nursery or schooling patterns. Women also found their care arrangements interrupted or swept aside when employers changed their shifts at short notice or left it to the last minute to inform them about contract renewals. This chapter presents and analyses the problems women had asking for consideration of their care responsibilities, and the demotions, pay cuts and dismissals that resulted for some. It explores the extent to which women were willing or able to negotiate care-friendly working conditions with or without knowledge of relevant employment rights. Where employers were flexible, the chapter explains how and gives some detail about how this helped workers.

Overall, this chapter supports the findings of previous chapters about the importance of women's status and contract type to their ability to disclose care or negotiate care-friendly work patterns. Yet it adds specific details about the stakes and outcomes of attempting to negotiate care. A key finding is that employers responded to the care obligations of their precarious workers as failings or impediments at best, and at worst, as a kind of "disobedience" or refusal to abide by the terms of their contracts. This explains the disciplinary action and dismissals taken against some workers. We have already seen that women feared being seen as unreliable or as "rocking the boat" by disclosing or attempting to negotiate around care obligations. Nevertheless, because care obligations were themselves dynamic, many of the women on the study found themselves having to negotiate around care either on a one-off basis or longer term. This chapter covers employers' responses to women talking about care, disclosing care obligations or formally or informally asking for flexible work. Chapter Seven then picks up on what the women did next.

Negative environments and responses

We begin with negative environments at work, in which generally inflexible employer responses and structural discrimination were sometimes accompanied by more severe action such as demotions, disciplinary action and dismissals. The following section then covers situations in which employers' responses were more positive or accommodating of women's care responsibilities, describing what employers did and the effect this had on women's ability to balance precarious work with care.

Generally inflexible

This category covers a range of informal practices that created a negative environment for women with care responsibilities but which did not always amount to something we would term 'disciplinary action' or worse. Interviewees experienced some of these practices as being to do with decision-making by individual line managers and others as being more to do with inflexible organizational structures, although it is clear that the two were interlinked.

The importance of line managers' responses was a key theme in women's accounts of managing care and work. So was scepticism about employers' intentions to provide family-friendly rights. This scepticism ranged from general concerns to more specific fears. For example, Nuala alluded to employers avoiding legal and policy restrictions on asking about children in interviews by simply assuming that most women workers had care obligations:

'I mean, all this rubbish about we can't ask you if you've got kids and they can't ask when you actually apply for a job. It doesn't matter whether they can ask you if you've got kids or not. If you are a certain age, the assumption is, you've already got kids'.

Yvonne, a cleaner, stated that even if better family-friendly rights were brought into force, academics in her university might benefit, but operational staff such as cleaners would not benefit.

Interviewees reported taking time to "size up the situation" before mentioning care obligations or trying to negotiate a different shift or working pattern with line managers. Linda, a customer service manager, tried to rearrange her shifts in order to care for her granddaughter. Her manager told her that "looking after your granddaughter is important for you, but it's not to the company". Line managers also often asked if other people could do the care, from partners to parents to other family members, which many women found distressing given the time they had taken thinking about and arranging care networks:

'The first thing they say is, "Is there no-one else?" Hang on a minute, have you sat and spoken to me about where my parents live? How many of us are in the family that can look after them? Sometimes there is only one person, because they've got no brothers and sisters or other relatives or they may live too far. The worst one we've had is when somebody said, well, she shouldn't have had kids'.

Interviewees also found themselves in situations where last minute time off or flexibility were needed due to an emergency or new care responsibility. In these situations, some line managers said that due to the contract a worker had signed, alterations to shifts for care reasons were not possible. According to Sandy, a retail worker: "I was told, you know, we don't care that you've got childcare issues. You signed a contract and you've got to come in".

Women were often upset or angry about line managers' negative responses and critical of their manager's reasoning. For example, Dipika's son was very ill and in need of specialist medical care. Dipika's line manager in her university job suggested Dipika take unpaid leave, which she took as a supportive suggestion at the time. However, she later became sceptical about it when she found out that colleagues had been given paid leave for similar situations. Sally, a retail worker, was called away from her retail job when her son split his head at school. She called her manager immediately to explain and was told she could go. Later, she updated her manager that her son needed stitches and was surprised when her manager asked her if she was returning for the last couple of hours at work. Sally felt it should be obvious that she could not leave her son.

Interviewees drew conclusions about employers' attitudes to care based on such experiences. Employer inflexibility at a time of considerable stress for these women was often interpreted as signalling that a similar response could be expected in future. For example, in the aftermath of her mother's unexpected death, Zoe was caring for her father, who had Alzheimer's, as well as two school-aged children. She was late for work a couple of times. Based on her employer's response, Zoe came to the conclusion that not only would her own manager be inflexible in future but the seasonal job she was doing, which represented a step away from claiming benefits, was not suitable for her circumstances:

'I realized very early on that there was no leeway given if you had children. My dad had Alzheimer's, and also he'd found my mother, my mother had drowned, and he tried to resuscitate her and he was just in a situation of trauma. A couple of days I'd been a bit late, because I had stayed to get my dad up and get him his breakfast. It had only been fifteen minutes. I'd been reprimanded and I said, "Well, the situation is quite difficult at the moment". They told me off and said, "If you start at ten you start at ten"'.

Even when women tried to plan ahead and negotiate a more appropriate shift pattern, line managers often refused, citing organizational reasons. Women felt sceptical about line managers' decisions, sometimes using their own knowledge of the organization and sometimes comparing themselves with colleagues, as we have already seen with Dipika. In another example, Kelly, who worked on a permanent very low hours contract in retail, tried to get shifts that would fit around her children's nursery and school times. She was told that her job was to cover dinners and her shifts could not be altered, however she could see other workers getting the hours they needed to fit around childcare needs.

Women interviewed for this study generally understood that organizational constraints might have a bearing on whether their care responsibilities could be taken into account. Yet an important theme was that employers should also make an effort to understand their circumstances instead of turning down requests without sufficient consideration. Organizational constraints took a variety of forms. Sometimes the employing organization was open and running at times when schools or childcare would have been closed, and women found it difficult to get the flexibility they needed to cover school or nursery holidays. However, in addition to holiday periods, workers often found weekly routines were not open to negotiation. Workers on short-hours permanent contracts in retail found it very difficult to vary their shifts, which were scheduled for evenings and weekends to cover long opening hours.

'My contract hours are 24. I work a Friday, a Saturday and a Sunday. They are the weekend shifts which nobody ever wants to swap or change. If I need a day off in an emergency it's really quite difficult'. (Sandy, retail worker)

'I've asked work if they can adapt my shifts so I can start later. It's not fair to keep [daughter] out three nights a week. I am trying to get her into a routine. But it's hard because the job role I am doing, the shifts are 6–12. So I have asked them if I can go on a different department, but they say that they can't create jobs'. (Fiona, retail worker)

A significant issue for retail workers was the increasing use by employers of 'just-in-time' human resource management strategies, which attempt to match the number of workers to locations and schedules more efficiently for the employer. Such systems make extensive use of forecasting, which created difficulties for women who previously took specific hours in order to cover care arrangements. Linda, a customer service worker, put it this way:

'You couldn't say then, "Can I do a 10 while 4 instead of a 9 while 3?", because they needed you. They could forecast when they needed you'.

When working shifts and hours are set to match with an employer's forecasted needs, it becomes much harder for workers to insist on care-friendly working arrangements. Interviews indicated that in very large retail organizations, human resource management and scheduling systems have become interlinked with stock management so extensively that workers feel that contracted hours are determined largely through forecasted needs, leaving much less scope for workers to negotiate family-friendly shift patterns. Tara described the effects of in-store stock management systems on the contracts of workers with care responsibilities, which, she said, could lead to dismissal if workers were not flexible enough:

'In-store stock management systems are linked to HR resourcing systems so they predict what they're going to need based on what's been purchased at similar times in the past ... So what happens with a colleague's contract is they will change it and so they will have a meeting and say, "Right, we've had a look and we don't need you in at eight o'clock on a Monday morning. But what we do want you to do is to work on a Saturday night". "Well, I can't work a Saturday night, because I look after my mum and dad", for example, or "I look after the grandkids for the weekend". "Well that's not good enough, because we need you there". After about three conversations they get 12 weeks' notice and their contracts are either changed or they are dismissed. And when that happens, you don't get a new contract'.

In interviews, women talked about the anxiety these systems and their associated human resources policies caused for workers who had carefully fitted their work schedules around their care networks, and vice versa. Combining short-hours or flexible contracts with stock management or other systems creates an environment for workers in which even pre-agreed working arrangements can be overridden on the basis of the flexibility needs of the employer. Natalie, a supermarket worker, put it this way:

'Even though you are flexible and you say at the interview, I can't do this day, I can do this time, the stores can still enforce it'.

Women working in retail contrasted such conditions with other jobs they had done. Sandy made a comparison between retail and manufacturing, her previous occupation, and suggested that manufacturing had provided more care-friendly working hours because they had a predictable period of shut down.

'I loved manufacturing. Monday to Friday and that actually was 9–5, then you would get the shut down and you will get time off for Christmas. So, more or less, all the school holidays were covered because you were off at the same time. It was more flexible when they were off for the six-weeks holidays. I think with retail, because they are so under-staffed and I know that's the case because I go round them all, [names of supermarkets]. They are grossly under staffed so they haven't got that degree of flexibility for their staff. When they tell you to come in, you have to be in'.

The interplay between line management and organizational policies and norms was very important. Retail workers were aware of employer policies on family-friendly working conditions that appeared very impressive but also said that the policies were not applied in individual situations, with problems arising at the level of store management:

'Companies are supposed to be caring, sharing, flexible. But when push comes to shove, they are not. At the top of the umbrella, the companies say one thing and when it gets down to store level, store managers say different things, so it's not consistent'. (Sam, retail worker)

'Head office were really good. The problem we have is head office will understand it. When it gets to the stores and the managers, it just breaks down. The whole system seems to break down at store level'. (Tara, retail worker)

As Tara explained, the yearly cycle for supermarkets features a busy period around Christmas and then a period in January where stores start monitoring sickness and reducing overtime. At other times in the year, customer trends change such that people shop later, meaning that supermarkets want people to work evenings. These periods of change create varying expectations of work hours that clash with care obligations, as well as leading to increased scrutiny by line managers. In this way, organizational issues ranging from the relationship between stores and head office, to in-store stock management, to fluctuating annual financial concerns could all shape line managers' attitudes to workers with care responsibilities, also sometimes leading to disciplinary action.

Structural discrimination

We saw in Chapter Two that structural race discrimination affected women's access to work and their pay rates. Another effect of structural inequalities is to create situations in which it is harder to balance care with work. Tina described herself as mixed race, had British citizenship and was brought up in South Africa. She and her partner wanted to have their baby in South Africa because her partner had South African citizenship and had already been refused entry to the UK on one occasion. They found out that due to nationality laws she had to be in the UK when she gave birth, otherwise she could not pass on citizenship to her baby. So Tina had her baby in the UK without her partner present, and they maintained their relationship over Skype until he was later able to join her. This had a significant effect on her working life, restricting the number of hours she could work, as well as her career progression. In this way, the interplay of immigration and nationality laws and family-friendly rights had a distinct impact on Tina.

Structural discrimination could undermine workers' ability to disclose a care obligation or negotiate care-friendly hours. Sally, a young retail worker from South London, described feeling that parents of her generation, class and geographical location were not taken seriously with regards to flexible work, leaving these workers open to greater control by employers:

'The way that young parents, especially, young parents and people within certain deprived areas are portrayed, I feel like if I did have an issue with a company surrounding flexible working, I feel like it wouldn't be taken seriously by anybody. Which is I think where companies feel they have so much control, because they constantly do stuff like this and nobody says, wait, no, you can't do that. That's against the law or that's against employment law'.

Another example is Yvonne, who experienced race discrimination in her cleaning job in a university. Yvonne's manager impersonated her Caribbean accent and blocked her from taking training to further her career. The manager also refused Yvonne's request for care-friendly work hours during school holidays, which was also a less busy time in the university. Yvonne said her manager had made her realize she was Black. She knew she was Black before but had not been conscious of it. She experienced severe depression as a result of what happened.

Donna was Brazilian and working as a temporary lecturer in a university on numerous contracts. She suspected that her rate of pay, and the rates of other non-British staff, were lower than those of British nationals. She had repeated problems with her employer and public bodies in proving she had a right to work in the UK, even when her documentation made this clear. Finally, Natalie said that her experience of coming to the UK from Antigua and first being in the country gave her an interest in law and access to justice. At the time of interview, she was working in a supermarket, volunteering at a legal advice centre and studying towards a law degree.

In these ways, structural inequalities and racist harassment shaped women's experiences of and approaches to work, increasing the level of managerial control in the workplace, blocking routes to balancing unpaid care with their jobs and leading to distress and depression. These women's experiences of precarious work and the lack of available family-friendly rights were exacerbated by structural discrimination, creating distinct problems for each of them. Such experiences prompted one woman at least to develop her legal knowledge and skills in advocacy as a response.

Demotion, disciplinaries and dismissals

Interviewees reported employer responses to their care responsibilities that included demotion, disciplinary action and dismissal. For example, as the extract at the beginning of this chapter shows, Sam was a team leader in her retail job when her husband had a stroke leaving him in need of round-the-clock care. Sam told her employer that due to her new extensive care obligation she would need to work 9 am–6 pm or 8 am–5 pm Monday to Friday. Her manager told her that the role of team leader meant that she needed to be flexible and work a shifting rota within a seven-day period. As a result, Sam was forced to step down to a general assistant role and take a pay cut.

Interviewees also reported being afraid of potential disciplinary action, which exerted a significant chill on women considering approaching employers to change shifts in situations of last minute or emergency care needs. Linda, a customer service worker, had multiple care responsibilities, including caring for her elderly mother who had dementia. Fear of disciplinary action led her to deploy strategies to help her concentrate on her work and hit her targets when she was worrying about her mother. Chantelle, a registered nurse, talked about being worried about taking sick leave for herself and her son when they needed it, because she was aware that taking too much sick leave could result in disciplinary action:

> 'They are so strict and so rigid. You have to do the shifts that you are given. I remember there were times when sometimes you call in to say, my son is not well and I can't come in. And then maybe you are not well yourself. If you call in sick three times in three months, you have to face a disciplinary'.

Sandy had two school-aged children and talked about how difficult it was to get time off for an emergency. Before she found out that she was permitted to work her hours at a different time, she was told that she would face disciplinary action for taking time off at short notice. Tara and her husband were disciplined for taking time off to visit her husband's elderly mother abroad when she was taken suddenly very ill. Despite calling and emailing to notify their employer of the reason for absence, and getting the agreement of their line manager, Tara and her husband were both subsequently given a written warning. Tara managed to appeal these warnings successfully but she found the process very stressful.

Sandy and Tara's experiences are examples of how employers can confuse sick leave with time off for emergency care reasons when recording absence, even where policy is to allow 'authorized absences' for emergency care. As one interviewee explained, human resources processes in large retail companies could be rigid even if they did allow authorized absence for care. Staff would often record absences as sick leave even when women explicitly notified the employer of a care-related reason, leading women to be given verbal warning for a certain number of absences.

The most serious outcome of disclosing a care responsibility or encountering a problem balancing care with work was dismissal. Dismissals happened at different stages in women's employment, from probation, to the non-renewal of a contract at the end of a temporary job, through to dismissal from an otherwise ongoing position. Termeh, a single mother, was unemployed at the time of the interview and had a seven-year-old son. She had lost a previous job in local government after failing her probation due to problems scheduling her son's drop-off around work:

'I had a bit of a problem with the manager, I was struggling at the time. I was trying to drop [son] off at the nursery and then rush all the way to the city centre, 'cause it was a bit further away now, the job. I spoke to my manager, you know, I asked instead of coming for nine o'clock is it possible I could come for quarter past nine or 9.30 and she was not helpful one little bit … She passed everybody's probationary period after the three months but she didn't pass mine'.

Mandy had a number of temporary contracts back to back at a university over five years. When she became pregnant, her contract was not renewed, leaving her out of work. A final example is Sharon, an agency care worker based in Liverpool, whose daughter had a disability requiring round the clock care. Sharon went for what she understood was a job interview with a care agency and mentioned at the interview that she would need to take a week away from work in the summer because her daughter had a hospital appointment in London. She brought the hospital letter with her as proof. The agency manager told her it would not be a problem, but when she came back from the week away, she was told her services were no longer required.

In summary, then, it is clear that some women who managed to get beyond their fear of "rocking the boat" experienced a range of negative employer responses. They encountered structural discrimination and/or low-level daily hostility to negotiating care, which consisted of refusals to alter shifts and inappropriate comments and questions about care obligations. These actions and attitudes of line managers combined to create an environment in which women feared talking about care or asserting their needs. On a broader institutional level, systems used by employers could skew workers' ability to gain care-friendly shifts. For those working in retail, an important theme was the interplay between stock management systems and human resources creating expectations that staff would be available despite care obligations.

Other employer responses to workers' changing or con-tinuing care obligations were more severe and included demotion, pay cuts, disciplinary action and dismissal. In all of these situations, employers framed a care-related action by a worker essentially as disobeying management or, in more severe situations, as breaking their contract with the worker. This 'care as disobedience' model could not have operated without the general background hostility to workers disclosing care that has already been outlined. The two ends of the scale were interlinked, even if the outcomes were apparently quite different for workers.

Positive responses

Women also, however, talked about ways in which their managers were flexible or supportive when it came to care-related requests. When work was described as genuinely flexible, it was because of the type of role, the general environment or specific employer policies. For example, part-time work on a temporary research contract suited Jane when she had a small child because she could choose her hours and reschedule work when her child was unwell. Bettina had a school-aged daughter and a mother with dementia and she was unsure about how to describe her contract for a care provider. However, what mattered to her about the contract was that it was "very flexible" around school holidays. Janice, whose son had a learning disability, worked for 13 years for Ann Summers, hosting parties. As she put it:

> 'It just fits around you and that's why I did it, because you work when you want to work rather than working when you have to work. So if you couldn't get a babysitter, you could go and do, you could give your party to somebody else. It just was easier'.

Dedicated informal or formal employer policies also made a difference to interviewees' lives. Termeh had previously held a temporary post in an office working for the city council. She enjoyed working in that role. The office had a formal 'flexi-hours' policy, which allowed workers to arrive late and leave early, as long as they were able to cover core hours meeting with members of the public. Informal arrangements could mirror or diverge from existing formal policies. For example, Tina talked with her line manager about making a formal request for flexible work under the university's policy but was told that it was "quite complicated". Instead, her line manager offered an arrangement whereby she could arrive half an hour later and leave half an hour earlier with no cut in pay. She was grateful for the arrangement and talked about feeling protected by her manager in a context in which "every little minute is counted in terms of how you are paid".

As well as the type or structure of work being flexible, women also talked about the important role their line managers played in helping them to manage work alongside care responsibilities. Women appreciated line managers being generally helpful and approachable. Linda, a customer service worker, described feeling confident about her manager because of her "whole persona":

'She smiles at you when she walks past and she doesn't know my name probably but she looks like she's a warm person. I would be all right about going to her if I needed to, but I never have'.

Katia had a good relationship of trust with her line manager in her research job, and was able to tell her about her ongoing challenges caring for her mother, who had severe mental health problems. This meant that when her mother committed suicide, Katia could have a conversation with her line manager about her specific needs. Termeh described her line manager in her city council role as "really understanding" and "very approachable" when she had to vary hours due to caring for her young son.

A positive and thoughtful response from a line manager was appreciated even when workers felt that, otherwise, a line manager may not have understood what they were going through. Sandy worked in retail, lived with a disability and had two school-aged children. She described her relationship with her line manager as being one where she could "sit down and talk to her" even if her manager might not immediately understand her situation.

A recurring theme was the importance of managers listening to workers, being approachable, understanding the workers' situations, knowing the policies and being proactive in altering policies if necessary. For example, women noted situations in which line managers had been instrumental in allowing them to respond to a care emergency through paid or unpaid leave at short notice. Termeh said that in her previous city council role, she could call at the last minute if her son was unwell and her line manager and colleagues would take over or rearrange her appointments. Bettina recalled a situation when her daughter's school had called her at work and her line manager had allowed her to go without "docking" her pay. Jane was happy that her line manager allowed her to take time off to go to doctors' appointments with her daughter and take it as holiday or make up the time later. Sada looked after her elderly mother alongside having a low-paid, informal child-minding role. When her mother was not well, she was able to take time off, but was paid less as a result.

Other examples of specific action to provide flexibility included restructuring temporary contracts. When Katia's mother died and Katia was caring for an infant daughter, her line manager restructured the temporary contracts she was working on so as to lengthen the overall period of employment and decrease her everyday workload. In the immediate aftermath of Katia's return to work after maternity leave and bereavement, her line manager ensured that she could focus on one thing at a time instead of performing tasks simultaneously, and scheduled more regular meetings to check in with how she was getting on.

A common perception was that when line managers were flexible, it was for personal reasons. For example, Natalie thought that it made a difference that her line manager was a single parent just like she was:

> 'Next week I've got parent's evening at school. I haven't seen my manager for the week now, but I know it's going to be okay 'cause she's a mum herself. She's a single parent so she would be ok with me'.

However, there were limits to the discretion that line managers could exercise, and again these limits related to organizational features of the employer. Natalie thought that she had more flexibility in her retail job because she worked in an office, but that when she had been working on the checkouts, her line managers could not be so flexible:

> 'Previously, it was a challenge. Someone on the checkouts, they can't just say, "I need tomorrow to leave early because of this, that or the other" because then they are the front end. But for me, because I work in admin, it's easier for me to do that. I think it depends on your job role, it varies'.

As well as different expectations for different roles, Natalie also talked about different types of stores. There was more pressure on line managers in an express or metro store than in a larger store to cover a wide variety of roles.

Despite these women all being in precarious work, it had been possible for managers to respond to their care obligations positively and often with constructive or creative approaches to employer policies. Personal warmth and approachability was particularly appreciated, perhaps helping workers to overcome their reluctance to "rock the boat". Workers noted the limitations on managers, including in retail, where the type of store or role within a store would constrain a manager's discretion. Yet the willingness and ability of managers to facilitate a care-friendly work environment had a positive effect and reduced the overall stress of balancing precarious work with care.

Conclusion

This chapter has focused on how employers responded to women's care responsibilities in precarious work. Interviewees described environments in which structural discrimination or daily low-level hostility had a chilling effect on their ability to disclose care obligations, with inappropriate comments made to care providers about who could do the care or which people should be the recipients of care, and refusal of informal requests without adequate consideration. They pointed out differences between employers' stated organizational policies around family-friendly care and the positions of line managers. The women also described organizational processes that made it harder for them to balance care and work: shift allocation systems based on forecasting and stock management, for example. When women encountered these issues they formed the view that such difficulties could arise again in future, which further constrained their ability to manage work and care. Some employer responses were more extreme, including demotion, pay cuts and dismissal due to women disclosing a new care obligation or even attempting to assert a previous agreement around care. These responses had immediate and long-lasting impacts on women's livelihoods, with some of the women still being unemployed at the time of interview.

A common theme running through these situations was that employers viewed care as at best an inconvenience, and at worst as disobedience. Whether it was the refusal of an informal one-off request or the failure to pass a worker's probation due to her request for flexibility, these employers constructed care as something that unjustifiably interfered with their business or breached the various types of precarious contracts on offer to these women. We have seen in Chapter Two that the women rarely took on precarious work out of choice, and Chapter Three has covered the fears these women had that they would not be able to stay in the jobs they had, especially if they disclosed a care obligation. While most jobs feature some imbalance of power between employers and workers, precarious work features an unusually large imbalance of power because employers have more extensive immediate control over women's ability to work. Combined with the assumption that care is almost akin to disobedience or a breach of the work contract, this creates a hostile environment for workers to negotiate care-friendly hours.

However, interviewees also reported situations in which they felt their employers facilitated or allowed care-friendly working. Women talked about formal or informal policies that managers used, or worked around, to help women cope with new or fluctuating care needs. An important theme was the approachability of line managers, the extent to which it was possible for women to build up relationships of trust with them, and the action they took when care-related needs emerged. Women reported specific examples when line managers helped them, including restructuring temporary contracts to allow time for care and recovery after a bereavement, paid compassionate leave and allowing time off for a care emergency without "docking" pay. Yet in those situations where workers encountered a positive response, it is possible that the high level of managerial discretion that is associated with precarious work was what made a difference. In other words, where shift patterns are under the control of the manager, it is possible for the manager to exercise this control in such a way as to be responsive to workers' care obligations. While this is a positive finding, indicating that with insight and goodwill it is possible to accommodate precarious workers' care needs, it also further highlights the extent to which the lives of precarious workers are influenced by the decisions and attitudes of their managers, a theme to which we return in the next chapter.

Key points

- When interviewees had to disclose a care responsibility to their employer, line managers' responses were extremely important, determining whether the employer would be flexible or not.

- Women encountered a range of 'generally inflexible' responses to their care responsibilities. These included asking if other people could do the care or making other negative comments.

- The interviewees understood that organizational factors might constrain employers' ability to offer care-friendly working conditions. However, women in retail jobs encountered particular problems with schedules determined through human resources strategies that were closely interlinked with sales forecasting and stock management.

- Structural discrimination and harassment relating to race, nationality, age and class further undermined women's ability to secure care-friendly work patterns, causing distress and depression.

- Women feared and experienced disciplinary action, demotion and dismissals due to raising a care responsibility at work.

- When employers' responses were positive, this was due to the overall shape of the job fitting with workers' care responsibilities, informal and formal policies and the approach of the line manager.

SEVEN

What Women Did Next

We have seen in Chapters Five and Six that women encountered a range of problems when disclosing care obligations at work. This chapter focuses on what the women did next. It explores how they found out about family-friendly rights, how they felt about their contracts and what actions they took. Despite all the differences in the women's jobs and their understanding of the law, every woman interviewed for this project talked about her contract and her boss. For this reason, a key theme in this chapter concerns women's bargaining power at work: the way that women's understanding of their contracts and relationships with their managers interacted with their wider circumstances and affected if, when and how they could negotiate at work.[1] Bargaining power was in large part shaped by the type of contract women had, so understanding the 'chill effect' of particular precarious contracts is important to understanding women's experiences at work more broadly.

Using this understanding of women's bargaining power, the chapter then describes what interviewees did when employers responded negatively to their requests or when their overall working environment was hostile to balancing care with work. This is important because on the whole, interviewees wanted

---

[1] In exploring what 'normal' people do when faced with conflict at work, this chapter is inspired by the methods and perspectives in Barmes, L. (2015) *Bullying and Behavioural Conflict at Work: The Duality of Individual Rights*, Oxford: Oxford University Press.

to remain in employment and so were faced with an immediate dilemma about how to reconcile competing demands. When they had more bargaining power at work, women asserted their rights, considered legal action or brought children into work. When women had less bargaining power, they absorbed the stress back into their home and care environment, took sick leave to cover care emergencies or they left their jobs.

Finding out about employment rights

We have already seen in Chapter One that many of the women interviewed for the study would not have been eligible to claim rights in order to request flexible work or take time off for family and dependents in an emergency, for example, because they were not 'employees' and/or they did not have sufficient time working with the employer. Indeed, the research project that led to this book started with the question of what women do when they are not eligible for family-friendly rights, as we know that such rights are only generally available to a narrow group of 'employees' and often do not cover precarious contracts. The question of interviewees' general responses to inflexible employers is covered later in this chapter. However, it is still important to understand how, if at all, women gathered information about rights that were available to them, or rights that were available to other people but not to them.

Interviewees reported little or no knowledge of employment rights in general or family-friendly rights in particular. When workers were aware of rights, there were two main routes for this knowledge: women's motivation to find out, driven by a particular situation at work, and previous experience or training. Sam explained that her own research into family-friendly rights came about when her husband had his stroke: "My husband had his first stroke in 2005. And before that … it didn't seem relevant if you know what I mean, because it didn't affect me. So once things start affecting me, then I need to find out where to go".

Once women realized they needed information about employment law, they consulted a range of sources, including online information, colleagues and union resources and training. Jane, a university researcher, described running Google searches and finding out on an official government website that students would not be eligible for maternity allowance. She then consulted online forums where she found that other women had the same problem as her, and that she would not be eligible because she had not worked the required length of time.

Interviewees who relied on colleagues for information did not report cross-checking the accuracy of this information with other sources, such as legal advice websites. In some cases, information from colleagues prevented a worker from trying to access rights. Zoe consulted colleagues in her seasonal job when her mother died and she had to take care of her father, who had Alzheimer's, alongside her two sons. She was told that she would not be eligible for compassionate leave and would have to take unpaid leave. As a result, she decided not to continue in the job. In other cases, information gleaned from colleagues opened up the possibility of flexible work. Termeh was having problems with dropping off her son at nursery and then getting to work. One of her colleagues was friendly with a manager who advised Termeh that she should be allowed to come in later if she had a child. And some women reported sharing information with other colleagues in such a way as to encourage them to assert rights. Sandy, a supermarket worker, made sure her colleagues knew they could swap or change shifts for care reasons.

Other sources of information about family-friendly rights included previous experience of family-friendly working environments or processes and union training. Yvonne remembered when flexible work was first introduced from her time working in a restaurant:

'That flexi-hours that they have, they introduced it when
it was Tony Blair. I remember when they introduced it.
I was flexible with the waitresses when they came in. The
first thing we asked them, how old is your child? What
pattern of work suits you?'

Unionized retail workers also demonstrated consistently high
levels of up-to-date legal knowledge, often gained through
union training, ranging from informal support through to a
diploma programmes in employment law. In interviews, these
women often referred to specific laws, contractual rights,
employer policies or agreements between employers and
unions. This level of specific knowledge allowed Tara, a retail
worker and union member, to liaise with her employer, changing a human resources IT system to prevent colleagues from
being disciplined for care-related absences. Unionized workers
also demonstrated confidence in asserting family-friendly rights
in disputes with employers about flexible working. As we will
see later in the chapter, Carol relied on her knowledge of legal
process regarding the right to request flexible work when
refusing to accept her manager's argument that "the needs of
the business" prevented him from allowing her to reduce her
working hours.

Contracts and bargaining power

We have seen from Chapter Six that women encountered
structural discrimination, general hostility and specific
problems such as demotion, disciplinary action and dismissals
in mentioning a care responsibility at work or attempting to
negotiating care-friendly working patterns. In theory, had they
been employed in their jobs long enough to gain access to
certain rights (for example the right to request flexible work,
to time off to care for family and dependents in an emergency,
anti-discrimination rights and protection against unfair dismissal), they could have addressed these issues by asserting such

rights.[2] In particular, some women could have made claims based on sex discrimination over working arrangements that looked neutral but which had a detrimental effect on their ability to provide care.[3] Others, such as Yvonne, could have made claims for racial harassment. However, due to the types of contracts these women had, they were discouraged from making a claim due to the fact that they did not think of themselves as employees, establishing employment status would be too difficult and they might not have been able to say they had been working long enough with the same employer for certain rights to take effect (such as the right to request flexible work). Furthermore, the right to unpaid time off in an emergency would not have been useful to women whose incomes were already uncertain. More importantly, women did not want to "rock the boat" with an employer, and any of these claims would have de-stabilized their positions at work. Women also did not report having the time or confidence to pursue legal action. When Sharon lost her care job, for example, she went

---

[2]   The right to request flexible work is available to employees with over 26 weeks' employment with the same employer. The right to request time off in an emergency is available, unpaid, to employees. Anti-discrimination rights do not have a minimum required period of employment and are available to a wider group of workers than is covered by the traditional definition of 'employee'. Agency workers (for example, cleaners) have had trouble relying on such rights to deal with discrimination in the 'end user' organization (is the organization who receives and directs the worker who is sent to them by the agency). Protection against unfair dismissal is available only to employees with over two years' employment with the same employer. See Citizen's Advice guidance, available at: https://www.citizensadvice.org.uk/work/rights-at-work/

[3]   Indirect discrimination is when a practice or policy that looks neutral has a detrimental effect on people with particular characteristics. It is prohibited by the Equality Act 2010. If an employee makes a claim for indirect discrimination, then an employer can try to make an argument that the policy or practice was justified. See Equality and Human Rights Commission guidance, available at: https://www.equalityhumanrights.com/en/advice-and-guidance/what-direct-and-indirect-discrimination#indirect

to the job centre for advice and focused immediately on how to apply for benefits to bring in even a very small income until she was able to find work again.

In other words, the existence of legal rights does not provide the full picture when it comes to women's experiences of law in the workplace. Many interviewees would not have been eligible for key statutory rights that are available to 'standard' employees. And while some women could have been eligible for certain legal rights, they did not access them because they did not know about them or they would not have felt comfortable asserting them, as we have seen from Chapter Five. Furthermore, even if women were not eligible for statutory rights, like the right to request flexible work, it was always possible in theory that they could make an argument to their employer that due to 'best practice' they should still get a similar arrangement. However, this would require a lot of confidence and a sense of security at work.

What women almost always reported either having or knowing about was a contract and a manager or boss. The types of contracts available to women were in the hands of the employers, and the women understood this. This section explores how the women's wider circumstances combined with the type of contracts they held to shape their bargaining power at work.

Normally bargaining power refers to the relative position of parties in a legal relationship with each other. As a term, it is often used to describe the working relationship or power dynamics between employer and worker.[4] In this book, the concept of bargaining power helps provide a detailed description of women's awareness and use of law in relation to their precarious contracts. A key point to emphasize here is that

---

[4] The Supreme Court has recognized the effects of unequal bargaining power on the employment relationship in two cases concerning the definition of 'worker' status: Autoclenz v Belcher [2011] UKSC 41 and Uber BV & others v Aslam & others [2021] UKSC 5.

women's bargaining power was shaped by care responsibilities and the relationship between care and work, not just the individual working relationship between employer and worker. So the way the term is used in this book is broader than the employment relationship. I recap the factors contributing to bargaining power here because they provide important detail. Interviewees' care responsibilities involved a large amount of intellectual, emotional and physical effort, often leading them to get up very early or go without sleep, perform sequential care tasks, work with very little "wiggle room" and manage complex scheduling tasks. Interviewees provided care for children and adults by creating and repairing care networks made up of family, friends, nurseries, schools and care workers. Using these care networks, women responded to changing and sometimes very uncertain work patterns with techniques such as "pass the parcel", asking adults to "step in" or by creating longer-term financial arrangements between adults.

At the same time, as we have seen, women in precarious jobs reported feeling like "second-class citizens" in their jobs, or "dogsbodies". They saw other workers being treated on better terms and this impacted on their sense of their own status at work. They assessed their chances before making requests for flexibility or turning down shifts. In their accounts of managing work alongside care, women often held managers' attitudes to be decisive. However, due to the types of contracts they held, many women had job uncertainty, not knowing if or when they would get another set of shifts or another temporary contract. Women also had uncertainty due to the last-minute nature of shift allocation in some circumstances. The need to secure ongoing or future work, combined with a sense of lower status, made them reluctant to disclose care responsibilities or assert themselves at work. "Care-fog" – a feeling of being overwhelmed, fragmented or out of control due to intense pressures of working and providing care – affected women at exactly the point when they could have otherwise tried to find out about their contracts, their rights or ways of improving their conditions at work.

All of these issues affected women's bargaining power. Yet within the workplace itself, bargaining power was also shaped by the type of contracts women had with their employers, and what they understood of these contracts. Depending on their experiences, women held different views on what a contract was, whether they held a contract of any type for the work they were doing, and whether they could practically or legally access family-friendly working. A common theme in the interviews was that the assumed force of law had effects on women that went beyond the technical dimensions of their contracts. In other words, women experienced employers' contracts, and what employers said about the contracts, as more powerful than they were legally, and this was connected with women's lower bargaining power.[5] It is to these different experiences of what a contract was and what contracts did that we now turn.

Zero-hours workers

Women working on zero-hours contracts believed that these contracts did not convey a legal status to them that would be of use in accessing care-friendly work. A prevalent perception was that zero-hours workers would not be able to negotiate flexible working. Indeed, workers often referred to themselves as not even having a contract, implying that these arrangements conveyed no rights at all. This understanding of zero-hours work could have been the result of workers not having the documents they would normally associate with a contract or indeed any documents associated with their working position.[6] Or it could mean that they associated a contract with being an

---

[5] Many thanks to an anonymous reviewer for Bristol University Press for helping me make this point more precisely.

[6] Employees and workers have a right to a written summary of their terms of employment. This includes agency workers and, depending on their circumstances, workers on zero-hours contracts.

employee, a status that they thought they did not have. Sharon stated that many of her colleagues had been working for months and even years "without a contract". She also spoke of herself as being without a contract:

'I don't mind doing it, don't get me wrong. It's just basically when you haven't got a contract. My son said to me, when you go back, are you going to get a contract this time or are they just going to use you again?'

Zero-hours workers who believed they did not have a contract also reported a belief that employers could dismiss them or their colleagues without notice or reason. This belief was sometimes down to personal experience. As we saw in Chapter Six, Sharon worked on a zero-hours basis for a company providing personal care in the home. She successfully requested time off to take her daughter, who had significant disabilities, to a pre-arranged hospital appointment in London. When she returned, she was dismissed without notice because of her time away with her daughter. However, workers could and did interpret contracts in ways that diverged from what employers were telling them about their employment status. The key to women regarding a contract as being zero hours appeared in part to be that these contracts looked "one sided" favouring the employer and did not "guarantee" them work.

The need to secure future work prevented women from turning down work on zero-hours contracts for reasons relating to care, as Nuala (a teacher in a prison) explained:

'When I first started at [place of work], I was on a cover contract, which is basically zero hours and it says that on the contract itself as well. So it says zero hours and basically they call you in when they want. You can say, no. But if you say no, you are not going to have any work'.

When asked whether she would consider raising her care obligations with her employer, Renuka, a retail worker for a high-street stationary chain, was emphatic that she could not do this, as we have seen from Chapter Five. Renuka also stated that she would rather not challenge her contractual status because she hoped to secure a permanent position:

'I would rather keep quiet about the contracts. And I'm hoping to be permanent and hopefully not on zero hour. Hopefully they'll give me a contract'.

It was largely correct that many of these workers *might* find it hard, practically or legally, to prove employment status, although any legal advisor would seek further information before concluding that an employment contract was not present. Yet these workers' sense of being outside of *any* protective legal framework or ability to negotiate went beyond the 'real' legal and practical situation. Interviewees' understanding of zero-hours contracts left them fearful even of informally requesting care-friendly working arrangements, creating very constrained conditions for them in balancing work and care.

Workers on temporary contracts and agency workers

Unlike zero-hours workers, the temporary workers interviewed for this project did not refer to their "not having a contract". This suggests that these temporary workers might have generally understood themselves to have some kind of contractual status, even if they were time limited. As a matter of law, some workers on temporary contracts could have been classified as employees and therefore able to benefit from family-friendly rights, although none of the respondents in this category expressly referred to themselves as employees. Like zero-hours workers, these workers felt that decisions about their future employment lay with their managers. Many workers were wary of "antagonizing" managers for fear of jeopardizing contract extensions, future contracts or possible permanent positions. Dipika, a careers advisor on a three-year contract, put it this way:

'If you haven't got a job, you haven't got any rights. And so, you know, basically, you've got to look to the decision makers to prolong your contract. You can't antagonize people too much'.

Workers on temporary contracts focused on the length and conditions of their current contract, as well as on securing 'better' – permanent – contracts to gain stability and more career enhancement options. Sometimes they attempted to negotiate better terms and conditions or flexible working arrangements. As we have seen from Chapter Six, Katia was employed on two fixed-term contracts when she experienced family bereavement, a relationship breakdown and depression. Her manager suspended work on one of the contracts and added it to the end of the first contract in order to reduce Katia's workload for a period.

Agency workers reported a view that they did not have a contract with the end-user company, but they were unsure about the extent to which they had a contractual relationship of any type with the agency. For example, Simone was about to begin an agency care-worker job, which she defined as permanent work. However, she was unsure about her con-tractual status with the agency. Agency workers do have rights to request flexible working in some circumstances.[7] However, Chantelle, an agency worker, did not report any knowledge of this and in any case described working beyond her contracted hours in order to impress the organizations she worked for so that they would request her through the agency in future.

In this way, women on temporary and agency contracts generally understood they had contracts, even if time-limited

---

[7] Agency workers can make a request for flexible working when they return from parental leave.

ones. Yet this knowledge was shaped by the practical need to secure future work, a need which in many cases was structured by the temporary nature of the contracts themselves. Dipika's statement that "if you haven't got a job, you haven't got any rights" encapsulates the resulting logic: this was employment status, of a type, but because it was time limited, the women were aware that without a job, their rights and the ability to negotiate around care would be irrelevant.

Workers on low-hours permanent contracts

Women with low hours permanent contracts referred to having more of a feeling of security, derived from the permanent nature of these jobs. As Fiona put it, the importance of having a permanent short-hours contract in a supermarket position was "knowing that my job is safe". Tina, a university lecturer, had been transitioned onto a fractional contract from an hourly paid role. While the fraction was very small and the pay too low, she thought the permanent nature of the contract was "advantageous".

Problems to do with the large-scale use of these contracts by retail businesses have been covered in Chapter Two. Interviewees reported not being able to find contracts of over 16 hours per week with supermarket chains. They also reported needing more hours to make ends meet, or treading a tightrope with how the contracts fitted alongside working tax credits. Women held very different approaches to the question of whether they had to accept the employers' terms and conditions, or whether they could negotiate. Workers in higher education sometimes focused on trying to increase the work available to them through getting more hours per week or a bigger 'fraction' of a full-time-equivalent post. For example, Tina had requested a larger fraction or, alternatively, that the university allow her to take voluntary redundancy, because the pay on her contract was too small to support herself and her family. However, for retail workers, the generic nature of the contracts available and the size of the organizations offering the contracts left women feeling there was little to negotiate at the outset of employment, or later. To these workers, a contract was something to be signed and not negotiated, as Fiona, a retail worker on a 16.5-hour contract, explained:

'It just states what they are looking for in the contract, like how many hours you get paid for. What they expect of you. And then, obviously, you have to sign at the bottom just to say that you agree with the terms and conditions and stuff'.

Interviewees reported feeling constrained about asking for changes in these contracts because they were the only type of job available and because the contracts were aimed at filling specific gaps in the businesses. Other financial and scheduling problems were associated with the length and timing of the shifts. For example, Kelly's shifts in a department store in the middle of the day were intended to cover lunches for other staff. But they did not match with nursery half-days, meaning that Kelly had to pay for full nursery days to accommodate her four-hour work shifts.

In summary, women on permanent, low-hours contracts felt that the permanence of the contracts gave them a degree of safety. Again, because they expressly talked about the safety alongside the type of contract, it is likely that these workers linked permanence to employment status, whether or not they understood the details of how this worked legally. Added to that was the practical point that the permanent nature of the position meant that they did not have to worry about securing future work with the employer on a regular basis. On the other hand, because the hours were often much fewer than workers needed, they struggled with money and wanted to negotiate more hours, with varying outcomes depending on the type or location of the employer. As Chapter Six demonstrated, retail workers experienced employer rigidity in relation to care-related requests for flexibility.

Multiple contracts

The reasons for women holding multiple contracts have been covered in Chapter Two. Women held different combinations of contracts, some including a permanent position alongside a zero-hours job, for example, and others fitting together multiple zero-hours or temporary posts. These women talked in more detail about their employer benefits, hourly pay rates and entitlements to sick pay and holiday pay than women holding only one contract. This is because women compared their multiple contracts and, in doing so, read or asked about them. For example, Nuala recalled from memory, in great detail, the holiday and sick pay on her current contract and what would be due under a fractionalized contract that had been proposed by her employer:

> 'I get holiday time which is 13 per cent of the overall contract over the year. Obviously, because we started in October, that's less. It works out less and you've got to times it by twelve and divide it by eleven. That's a bone of contention ... Now if I go on a fractionalized contract, the fractionalized contract will give you up to 46 days a year, which still includes them holidays that the prison take and the shutdowns. But, obviously it would give you time. It would give you more holiday and you get sickness benefit as well and actually the annualized contract does give sickness benefit as well'.

By contrast, Donna held multiple short-term contracts for teaching and found the details of the diverging pay scales very difficult to understand. She addressed this by going into the pay office with her payslip and asking staff to explain each one to her. Therefore, in addition to the knowledge of law that women would have gained from each type of contract (permanent low hours, zero hours, and so forth), women on multiple contracts had a questioning and comparing approach to questions of pay and benefits. Often, this was centred around being able to fit jobs together around a care obligation. For example, Bettina held a permanent part-time job as a warden in a sheltered living facility and found it hard to save up holiday leave to look after her young daughter in the summer holidays. Her zero-hours contract as a relief carer gave her more flexibility in the holidays.

To summarize, women's understanding of their own contracts were central to their bargaining power at work. A common theme of the interviews was that the women were intensely aware of how much they could negotiate, if at all, with their managers. Employers controlled the types of contracts available to women, and these contracts created intensified power for managers in giving or withholding work. As we have seen in Chapter Five, this contributed to women's fear of "rocking the boat" with a request for care-friendly hours because the most important thing was to stay in work. Perceptions of whether a contract was negotiable were different depending on the type of contract women held and the sector they worked in. Agency workers and workers on low-hours permanent contracts felt less confident about the possibility of changing hours to fit with care responsibilities. Women on multiple contracts demonstrated a questioning and comparing approach because of the need to fit contracts together around care. Yet behind all of these differences lay the importance of managerial discretion, which could accommodate a care responsibility, on the one hand, or lead to a worker losing her job, on the other.

What women did next

We have seen that interviewees' bargaining power was shaped by many factors, including their previous and ongoing experiences at work, their care responsibilities and care networks, their understanding of their contracts and their managers. All of these factors also affected what women did when they were faced with a negative working environment or a manager's refusal to accommodate a care obligation. Women's strategies are clustered into two general groups in this section: responses in situations where women had less bargaining power in the workplace, and responses when women had more bargaining power on a temporary or long-term basis. Within each group of responses was a range of strategies, and women often used one or more strategies, sometimes from different groups, depending on their changing circumstances. Women's approaches ranged from absorbing the stress (which could otherwise seem like "doing nothing"), taking sick leave, refraining from using available policies or rights or leaving the job, to more confident strategies including taking a child to work, educating others about the dangers of using sick leave and asserting legal rights.

Less bargaining power

Absorbing the stress and going into work

We have seen from Chapters Three and Four that women routinely put significant effort into providing care, sometimes around last-minute shift allocations, as well as creating and repairing complex care networks. Women used techniques such as passing care responsibilities between multiple adults and care providers ("pass the parcel"), asking people to "step in", sleeping over at the houses of frail parents and shared scheduling, alongside durable medium- and longer-term care arrangements involving large financial decisions (for instance, who should claim carer's allowance, what job a woman should do to fit around school holidays) and multiple adults (adult children, partners and ex partners, for example).

When women reported having less bargaining power in the workplace, a common strategy was to absorb the problems associated with inflexible or unfriendly working arrangements. As such, inflexible precarious work could impact in more pronounced ways on women's own personal lives or their care networks. This could give the impression to colleagues and managers that tensions between work and care were not there or had been magically resolved. Yet such tensions would have inevitable effects on wider networks of people. For example, when Sam's shifts were changed in her supermarket job, she had to liaise with care workers and her daughter who claimed carer's allowance to look after Sam's husband, and she was worried that her daughter's care arrangements with her own children would be affected.

Taking sick leave

Women reported taking sick leave to cover care emergencies. Indeed, when women talked in their interviews about sick leave, it was usually connected to last-minute care issues. The types of jobs women were doing had a bearing on whether and how they could claim sick leave and whether they had access to statutory or contractual sick leave and pay. Women's thoughts and knowledge about sick pay varied. Nuala said she had never had a day's sick leave in her life, with the implication that she was proud of this record. However, when she talked about sick leave, she was describing a "rubbish" job as a cleaner on minimum wage and said she would not have known what the policy was.

When women believed they had no access to sick leave, unsurprisingly they did not report using it to cover a care emergency. Instead, they presented at work even when they were unwell. For example, Catherine, a teaching assistant, said she felt that she had to go into work whether she wanted to or not, because otherwise she was not going to be paid. She often experienced migraines and went into work regardless.

Similarly, Bettina, a care worker, said that with one of her jobs she did not get contractual sick pay and said that if she didn't work, she did not get paid. Neither Catherine nor Bettina talked about having enquired whether they were eligible for statutory sick pay. Linda, a customer service worker, said that she had "not really looked at my contract in a while" but thought that the requirement was to "always turn up", and that lateness and sickness were frowned upon. None of these women reported using sick leave, to cover for a care emergency or otherwise.

When women did take sick leave to cover a care emergency, it was because they knew sick leave was an option and felt they had no alternative but to draw on it in these circumstances. Yvonne was a part-time cleaner and said that her employer preferred for workers to call in sick when they had to cover childcare at the last minute. When asked why this was, she replied: "That is the only way the person is going to get [the leave]". Sandy said that many of her colleagues in her retail job were taking sick leave to look after children who were ill "because we thought we didn't have a choice".

As is clear from these examples, when women took sick days to care for children or attend important care-related meetings, it was because they believed that employers would not otherwise allow them to take time off. Most women (with the exception of Sandy) did not report knowing about the right to reasonable time off work to care for family and dependents in an emergency. And in any case, women's narratives of their working environments suggest they did not feel safe enough to disclose a care-related need for the time away from work. Women feared having an argument with a manager or "repercussions" if they disclosed the real reason for the time off. As Sandy put it:

'Some people they would ring in sick, because they think, I am going to have a row or they know that there is going to be repercussions when they go back into work'.

The extent to which women felt the need to justify their time off as sick leave rather than disclose their care obligations can be illustrated using Kelly's experience. Kelly worked in retail and said that she did not have access to paid sick leave through her contract. She had previously been very ill during a pregnancy, such that she had to take three weeks off work. She had thought she was going to get contractual sick pay during this illness, but found out that she was ineligible due to her working hours in the preceding months. Kelly had been informed about the possibility of claiming statutory sick pay but felt "going through all of the forms" was too onerous and instead relied on borrowing money from a relative, which still left her with very little to live on. When Kelly was later called into her child's school for appointments she described feeling like she had little choice but to risk claiming sick leave:

> 'You might have a really important place to go to, to do with your children and might have to go to a really important appointment in the school, and they won't accommodate for that. So then you've got to basically phone in sick. Even though you may not be sick. You've got to do it because your children, well, my children come first'.

Even though Kelly had experienced problems claiming sick pay in the past, she still took sick days to cover care responsibilities. In this way, understanding how women thought about and used sick leave is important for understanding how they negotiated care in situations where they felt under immediate pressure and thought that they had few rights otherwise to claim time off. The use of sick leave by precarious workers to cover care emergencies is a useful indicator of how much power they think they have to assert care-related needs at work.

Deciding not to draw on rights or widespread 'good practice'

When women had negative experiences disclosing or nego-tiating care, it discouraged them from asserting rights they knew about, whether these were rights in their contracts, general employer policies, statutory rights or involved asking the employer to honour wider principles concerning family-friendly working. This was exacerbated by an often already-existing fear of reprisals associated with their precarious status in the workplace. These women had some knowledge of family-friendly rights, such as the right to request flexible work, whether or not they applied to them individually as workers. When they saw or experienced employers failing to comply with the right or use good practice, this discouraged them from asserting any available rights or practices as new situations arose.

For example, Sally, a retail worker, had already experienced problems with her employer, when she was asked at very short notice to work in a different location. This made it very diffi-cult for her to then pick up her son from school. She had also experienced a lack of understanding from a manager when her son had been hospitalized with a minor head injury. Due to these experiences, and her status as a young single parent working in a deprived area, Sally was sceptical about asking for flexible work because it "wouldn't be taken seriously". A key issue with asserting rights was lack of enforcement:

> 'They constantly do stuff like this and nobody says, wait, no, you can't do that. That's against the law or that's against employment law'.

Leave the job

In all examples in this study where women left their jobs due to not being able to negotiate care-friendly working, the women found themselves either unemployed or in jobs with less formal legal protection than before. For example, Sherene was working as a teaching assistant when her mother was diagnosed with breast cancer. Due to the intensity of her mother's treatment, Sherene left her job and began claiming jobseeker's allowance. At the time of interview she had started work again, this time as a care assistant working for an agency. She said that if this happened again, she would stay in work and find a paid carer to look after her mother or relative

'because the previous experience I learned … I should continue to work and move the shift, or ask my company to take the family as a client and they send someone else as well to look after … my mother'.

Chantelle left her permanent job in a nursing home when her request for flexible working was turned down. She came to the conclusion that agency work would provide her with more flexibility. At the time of interview, she was working night shifts, and studying and caring for her children during the day. She said her pay was much better but she struggled with finding time to sleep and worked over and above her usual duties in order to secure future shifts.

More bargaining power

When women had more bargaining power, their strategies were different to those described in the previous section. They brought their children into the workplace when they could not find other ways of looking after them. They refrained from using sick leave and advised others to do the same. They dropped their hours, asserting the "needs of the family" against employers' arguments about the "needs of the business" when necessary, and they considered taking legal action against their employers.

Bringing children to work

Tina had a fractional contract as a lecturer with a very low income. As we have seen in Chapter Four, Tina described feeling too overwhelmed at times to question the basis of her new fractional contract. However, she also talked about taking her young son into the workplace when she found it difficult to arrange care for her children around her husband's work. For Tina, the difficulties of having her son with her at work were partially offset by the hope that this would help make childcare more visible. Natalie's situation was different, however. She was working as a checkout assistant in a supermarket when her youngest child was still at breastfeeding age. There was not enough time for Natalie to get home, breastfeed and get back to work on her breaks, and so Natalie's husband brought their daughter into the store to be fed when Natalie was on later shifts. For Natalie, having her daughter brought into work was not a positive reclaiming of work space. Instead, it underlined how difficult it was for her to manage care alongside her job.

Refraining from sick leave

An alternative narrative about taking sick leave for care reasons was that it could lead to disciplinary action and that it should be avoided. This perspective on sick leave was generally, although not exclusively, advanced by trade union members. Sandy was a trade union representative and described knowing that many colleagues who were working mothers called in sick when their children were unwell, for example, or when they needed to cover other care-related needs. She made the connection between using sick leave for care and a worker's overall absence record, stating that her employer would give three warnings and then dismiss a worker for repeated absences. She warned colleagues not to call in sick for this purpose. Similarly, Tara described educating her colleagues about the need to specify a care emergency when, due to the last-minute and very stressful nature of these situations, they might otherwise be tempted to simply call in sick. Tara's employer had a software system for recording absences with a drop-down menu that could specify 'no disciplinary' if absence was for care reasons. This was often not used if staff were not trained properly in recording absences. Tara described struggling to make sure that 'return to work' forms had correct information so that they would not lead to workers being disciplined.

Dropping hours

Making a request to drop hours was not widely reported, and indeed many women reported that the idea of having fewer hours and therefore a lower income would be very challenging. However, the women who did report dropping hours were not on high incomes to start with. Their reasons included facilitating care for an elderly relative, spending more time with an infant and recovering from a bereavement alongside coping with mental health problems. Carol had worked full time in a supermarket for ten years. When her mother-in-law became ill with Alzheimer's, Carol was instrumental in providing and coordinating care for her to such an extent that she would often get up at five in the morning or earlier in order to care for her before her shift started. Carol became exhausted and isolated and realized that she needed to make a change. She was eventually able to drop her hours after an initial request to her line manager was refused. She said that having the reduced time at work helped her get "the old me back ... instead of somebody that's trying to juggle everything at once". This was a profound source of joy for Carol. At the time of interview, she said that she and her husband were managing better than they had done. For example, it was easier to take her mother-in-law to hospital appointments and Carol was less tired overall and had more of a social life. She wanted to drop another day's work but did not know whether they could afford it.

Asserting "needs of the carer or family"

Women also reported using arguments that turned employers' stated reasons for not being flexible on their head. At the time of interview (and despite changes to the law, this is still the case), employers could legally turn down a formal request for flexible work by stating that the request could not be accommodated due to the "needs of the business". Retail workers like Sam talked about stating the "needs of the carer" back to line managers in a way that subverted the usual legal wording in support of carers' rights:

> 'The trouble is, the government can bring in whatever legislation they wanted, because there is flexibility now. But it doesn't necessarily mean that the company has to agree to it because they say – it's needs of the business. It might be their needs of the business but it's not our needs as a carer'.

We have just seen that Carol managed to drop her hours working in a supermarket. In fact, Carol had to fight for this. Her line manager turned down her initial request. When he went on holiday, Carol went above his head and got agreement from the next manager up in the hierarchy. On his return, Carol explained her action by stating her "needs of the family":

> 'I said: "I've dropped my hours". I said: "Needs of the family". He looked at me and said: "I don't understand what you mean". I said: "You say it's needs of the business and I say it's needs of the family". There was nothing he could do because it had already been processed'.

Asserting legal rights

Workers who were confident about their knowledge of legal rights demonstrated scepticism about managers' silence on the subject of family-friendly working and their knowledge of law, and considered asserting legal rights when necessary. Sandy said she believed that employers purposefully did not tell her colleagues about their entitlement to some family-friendly rights for fear of upsetting the rota:

> 'That I have learned, they will not tell me anything at all with your rights to time off and your maternity, even though the law says that you've got a right to flexible working. They don't tell you these things, because they just want you on a rota for the day you are rota'd in and the time and that's it'.

Women also said that managers often did not understand employer policies around family-friendly working. This meant that even if a woman found out about a law or policy and asserted it, she might have trouble gaining agreement from the manager. As Tara put it: "The problem we have is that managers don't understand what the law is. They don't even understand their own policies". Finally, Sam gained confidence through training in employment rights and her union membership. In response to changes in shifts that would have left her and her care network struggling to cope, Sam told her management that "if you want to get rid of me because of my caring responsibilities, I will see you at tribunal".

Conclusion

This chapter has considered what women did next when they encountered a problem balancing precarious work with care. It has advanced a broad definition of bargaining power as a way of understanding how women responded to workplace difficulties. Bargaining power was affected by women's daily routines, care networks, second-class work status and fear of reprisals, as well as by their strategies and moments of confidence. It was also affected by the types of contracts women were given and the attitudes of their bosses. When managers created formal or informal rules about recognizing care in the workplace, these rules were just as important to women in their everyday lives as "proper" laws would be; for example, the statutory right to request flexible work. Indeed, managers were able to act in the way that they did because they were relying on contracts that their businesses had set up. These contracts could have the effect of subverting many of the rights that are available to standard employees, but they also resulted in large imbalances of power between workers and employers that created a chilling effect when it came to employees negotiating care-friendly working arrangements.

The interviews conducted for this project indicate that when women lacked bargaining power in the workplace, they absorbed the stress of managing care alongside work, negotiating with their care networks (if they had them) along the way with varying levels of success. This could have the result of rendering the care invisible to the employer, giving the impression that any conflict between care and work had disappeared, when in fact the tension had simply been carried over into the women's wider care networks, away from the workplace. Other courses of action included taking sick leave (with an associated risk of disciplinary action), deciding not to assert rights the women knew they had and leaving a job or seeking alternative work. When women had more bargaining power at work, they dropped their hours, brought children to work, used statutory entitlements to emergency leave instead of taking sick leave, argued with employers about how the "needs of their family" should give them flexibility at work, asserted their legal rights and considered legal action.

Employers have a choice about whether to create the kinds of contracts that mean workers are eligible for statutory rights to family-friendly working. They also have a choice about whether to create and enforce their own standards of family-friendly working, no matter what types of contracts they use or workers they employ. When employers view care obligations as inconvenient or creating disobedience in their precarious workforce, this is because they themselves are creating the rules – or 'lived laws' – that workers have to cope with. With these insights in mind, we now turn to the final chapter, which draws on the findings that have been covered so far to address the question of how to provide family-friendly rights for precarious workers.

Key points

- Women generally reported little or no knowledge of employment rights in general or family-friendly rights in particular.
- The most important area of law that women thought about on a daily basis was their contract with the employer and their relationship with their manager.
- Women's bargaining power at work was shaped by their wider circumstances, including their care responsibilities and the type of contract they held.
- Zero-hours contract workers believed that these contracts did not convey a legal status to them that would then be of use in accessing care-friendly work.
- Temporary workers knew that decisions about their future employment lay with their managers and for that reason were wary of antagonizing them by raising a care responsibility at work.
- Women on short-hours permanent contracts felt prevented from asking for care-friendly working conditions because these jobs were the only type of job available and/or because the contracts were aimed at filling specific gaps in the businesses.
- When women lacked bargaining power in the workplace, they absorbed the stress of managing care alongside work, took sick leave (with an associated risk of disciplinary action), decided not to assert rights they knew they had or left their jobs.

- When women had more bargaining power, they dropped their hours, brought children to work, used statutory entitlements to emergency leave instead of taking sick leave, argued with employers about how the "needs of their family" should give them flexibility at work or asserted their legal rights.

EIGHT

Care-Friendly Rights for Precarious Workers

'I think there needs to be something that recognizes low paid workers for how they are treated. I can't work from home. I don't have that – I could technically set up a till in my house. You aren't going to bring your shopping to me to be scanned'. (Tara, supermarket worker)

This book has drawn on interviews with women in precarious work to understand how they managed work alongside unpaid care. While the women's accounts were diverse, a story has emerged about how and why this balancing act is so difficult and what could be done to support these women in the future with family-friendly rights. This final chapter recaps the key findings before outlining some considerations that could shape future attempts to provide family-friendly rights for precarious workers.

Summary of findings

Analyzing the accounts of work and care that women provided in their interviews, powerful themes have emerged about the lack of choice, low and fluctuating pay levels, fear of reprisals, imbalance of bargaining power and intensified managerial control that they experienced in precarious jobs. We have seen in Chapter One that the women did not choose precarious work but took it because other work in their chosen field or in their local area was not available. When the women started work, they had little power to negotiate care-friendly work patterns. Employers determined the rate of pay and set the timing and patterns of work. Making ends meet was difficult, and women used a range of strategies to make their money last until the end of their pay period, including paying attention to food and transport costs, borrowing, and selling items if they needed to. All of this had an effect on their ability to negotiate with their employers. It meant that the women needed to prioritize getting immediate or future work to secure their ongoing income.

This would all be enough of a problem if women came to their jobs without any other responsibilities, but Chapters Two and Three focused on women's responsibilities regarding providing care for loved ones. Care was often invisible to employers, but it structured the women's daily lives, finances and longer-term planning in important ways. Chapter Three gave a description of the care that women provided for children and adults, with many women undertaking multiple care responsibilities. Women described going without sleep, getting up early, performing care and work with little "wiggle room" in between tasks, moving between homes when necessary and putting intense effort into scheduling. They could feel overwhelmed by the combination of care and work, describing themselves as "headless chickens", "robots" or "machines". Chapter Four then described how women coordinated care networks with other people and with organizations (nurseries, schools) in order to make themselves available to do their jobs. Again, this effort was invisible to employers, yet when employers sent out or changed shift rotas at the last minute, or asked a zero-hours worker in the morning to do an afternoon shift, this would have effects on a wide range of people and care providers. Depending on who was involved in the care network and the needs of the person receiving care, women used strategies such as "pass the parcel" or "tag teaming" to provide care for children, or had other adults "step in" to assist them. They also made longer-term arrangements with other adults concerning jobs, care roles and finances. Nurseries and schools presented problems for women, including inflexibility related to booking and paying for nurseries alongside variable or low-hours shifts and the lack of care cover during evenings, weekends and school holidays. Essentially, these chapters showed how the women acted as a 'buffer zone' between care and work, resolving problems, coming up with solutions and often having to make big decisions with potentially long-term financial and emotional effects.

With all this in mind, it is not surprising that interviewees reported not wanting to "rock the boat" when it came to mentioning a care responsibility to an employer. While women often enjoyed their jobs, Chapter Five showed that they also felt like "second-class citizens" at work. Job uncertainty and last-minute shift allocations, as well as the women's lower status in the workplace, left them fearing reprisals if they talked too much about care or made requests. Added to this was the experience of "care-fog" – feeling overwhelmed due to the intense pressure of providing care alongside work – just at the point when it was necessary to get to grips with their contracts. Some women got confidence from being in a union and did manage to negotiate care-friendly working. However, overall, their need to secure ongoing work and their fear of being seen as unreliable combined to make it very difficult to disclose care responsibilities at work.

When it became impossible to hide a care responsibility – for example, due to a care arrangement breaking down or a loved one's suffering a health emergency – the response of the line manager was very important. Positive responses by managers included restructuring temporary contracts to provide a longer but less stressful period of employment, or simply being approachable when women needed to ask for time off due to school or hospital appointments. Line managers created a hostile environment when they asked if someone else could do the care, defined 'family' too narrowly or made other dismissive or undermining comments about women's care responsibilities. This was exacerbated by structural discrimination in the workplace and by racist harassment, for example. Women also feared, and some experienced, disciplinary action, demotion or dismissal for raising care-related problems at work. Negative and discriminatory responses by employers created the impression that women's care-related issues were akin to a kind of "disobedience" or in some way constituted their failing to fulfil the terms of their contract.

At this point, a question might normally be why these workers did not make a formal request for flexible work or assert other employment rights. Chapter Seven picks up on this point. Many employment rights to family-friendly working are simply not available to precarious workers. Such rights are designed for standard employees and they tend to exclude women in precarious work. These rights often require people to know that they are employees, which is a distinct type of employment status only available to some. They also often require a period of qualifying employment that can be as long as 26 weeks, or 6.5 months, which would be difficult for many people on intermittent or short-term contracts to reach, especially when the power to dismiss is in the employer's hands. The right to make a claim for unfair dismissal is only available to employees with more than two years in the same job. While many women in the study could in theory still draw on discrimination rights, this would require their having the confidence to raise a grievance and bring a claim against their employer in an employment tribunal, which would be very difficult to do alongside keeping their job. More importantly, the women interviewed for this project did not report knowing about, or asserting, employment rights on the whole.

In fact, as Chapter Seven shows, the most important aspect of employment law that the women interviewed for this study knew about was their contract. And when they talked about their contracts, some important themes emerged. Women on zero-hours contracts generally thought these contracts did not give them any right to family-friendly working. Temporary workers wanted a contract renewal and were wary of raising issues of care with their employers. Women on permanent short-hours contracts were aware their contracts were filling gaps in the workplace or in other people's schedules and did not feel they could ask for flexibility. Women's interpretations of their contracts combined with all the experiences they had with managing care alongside work to help create their bargaining power – the degree of power they had in the workplace as compared with their employer. Importantly, this study considers women's experiences and strategies for managing care as a core part of their workplace bargaining power, along with their contracts, what they thought about their contracts and the level of managerial control in the workplace. Separating out care from work would undermine a key finding of the study: that unpaid care and precarious work are dynamically interrelated. A last-minute change in a shift allocation could affect the careful arrangements between people in a care network, for example, and a new care responsibility could affect a worker's ability to work outside regular hours.

When women had little bargaining power, they responded to employer inflexibility by absorbing the stress back into their own lives and their care networks, they took sick leave to cover care emergencies, refrained from asking for 'best practice' around family-friendly rights or asserting any rights they did know about, and in some cases they left their jobs. When women had more bargaining power, they dropped their hours if they needed to, they brought children to work or engaged in other practices to break down the distinction between work and care, they used their statutory right to time off in an emergency (if they were eligible), they argued with employers about the "needs of the family" instead of the "needs of the business", and they considered legal action.

What does this mean for family-friendly rights?

The legal scholar Lydia Hayes has observed that 'when law at work entrenches hierarchies of gender, it does so on the basis of class'.[1] While social class is a complex phenomenon, it is clear that at present, family-friendly rights are not inclusive of all women. Precarious workers have reason to feel like second-class citizens. This book has highlighted several important gaps in family-friendly employment laws that have the effect of formally excluding women in precarious work or making it too difficult for them to draw on their rights. Let's take the right to request flexible work. This is only available to employees with 26 weeks or more in employment. It is not usually available to agency workers. This right is asserted by making a formal request to an employer. The kinds of problems that precarious workers have with this right include not knowing whether they are employees, not being employees, not being in work long enough to qualify and the risk of reprisals for requesting flexible work. Women interviewed for this study did pay attention to the type of contract they had, but they did not report knowing their employment status, and for the most part they did not report knowing about this right. If they had known about it, then, drawing on the findings from Chapter Five, it is likely they would not have wanted to "rock the boat" by claiming it.

Another example, which is much more widely available, is the right to time off to care for family and dependents. This is available to employees and provides unpaid time away from work to deal with emergencies involving dependents. Again, women in precarious work would not necessarily know their employment status. Women interviewed for this project experienced financial difficulties on very low pay to start with,

---

[1] See Hayes, L. (2017) *Stories of Care: A Labour of Law: Gender and Class at Work*, London: Palgrave.

and so the unpaid nature of this time off would make it difficult to claim. And as this study has shown, not knowing that they are eligible for this right, women sometimes take other routes, such as using up sick leave, which puts them at risk of disciplinary action.

Women in precarious work take contracts that are determined by their employers, are difficult to negotiate, involve set pay and which lead to situations of high managerial control and discretion in which women's bargaining power is impaired from the outset. Family-friendly rights are designed to benefit employees in permanent employment in situations where there is much less imbalance in bargaining power. What would it look like, then, to design family-friendly rights for precarious workers? Drawing on the research undertaken in this study, and particularly on women's accounts of balancing precarious work and care, the following seven principles and actions could guide our response.

Support measures to outlaw precarious work

Precarious contracts undermine women's bargaining power in the workplace and constrain their ability to disclose care responsibilities or arrange care-friendly working. For that reason, improving the conditions of precarious workers means supporting measures to outlaw zero-hours contracts, provide guaranteed hours and improve the position of temporary workers and those on involuntary part-time contracts, as have been suggested by the Institute of Employment Rights (in their 'Manifesto for Labour Law'), the TUC (Trades Union Congress) and the Low Pay Commission, among many others.[2] Yet even if such measures were implemented, we would still need to pay attention to how rights are targeted, making sure

---

[2]   See further: Institute of Employment Rights (2016) 'Manifesto for Labour Law'. Available at: https://www.ier.org.uk/manifesto/

Also see the TUC's campaign 'Control over when you work', accessible at: https://www.tuc.org.uk/FlexibilityAtWork

that any new system does not replicate the problems associated with the standard employment relationship that were covered in Chapter One. And in the meantime, providing effective rights to care-friendly working for precarious workers should be a priority. Precarious workers shouldn't have to wait for family-friendly rights.

Make employment status irrelevant to family-friendly rights

Most people do not wait for a contract of employment before taking on a care responsibility. Precarious workers are not usually in a position to negotiate their terms and conditions of employment when they take on a new job. Making family-friendly employment rights dependent on employment status leaves precarious workers without protection in circumstances where they have little or no control over their contracts. While the circumstances of each type of job are different and may require distinct approaches, it should not be the case that workers on precarious contracts are excluded or discouraged from claiming rights on the basis of decisions made by employers about how to structure their workforce. For these reasons, precarious work should be conceptualized as a form of 'contracting for work', one result of which would be that a much wider range of workers, contracts and employing parties would be included under legal regulations than is currently the case.[3] Introducing a single status of 'worker' to cover all working people apart from those who are genuinely self-employed is a powerful solution to the problem of improving the rights of precarious workers with care obligations. This

---

Finally, see the Low Pay Commission (2018) *A Response to Government on 'One-sided Flexibility'*, available at: https://assets.publishing.service.gov.uk/government/uploads/system/uploads/attachment_data/file/765193/LPC_Response_to_the_Government_on_one-sided_flexibility.pdf

[3]   Dukes, R. (2019) chapter 1, fn 20 at p 406; Fredman, S. (2004) chapter 1, fn 19.

suggestion by the Institute of Employment Rights would see workers protected by employment rights if they: (a) seek to be engaged by another to provide labour; (b) are engaged by another to provide labour; or (c) where the employment has ceased, were engaged by another to provide labour.[4] This kind of reform would help level the playing field between employees and precarious workers when it comes to family-friendly rights.

Aim for 'care-friendly' rights instead of 'flexibility'

Much current law, policy and best practice in the area of family-friendly rights assumes that flexible working benefits all women with care obligations. Yet this is not the case. The overwhelming assumption that flexible work is a solution to family-friendly working assumes a professional office-based employee with a high degree of autonomy over her work, a friendly (enough) boss and a permanent contract. Yet the rhetoric of flexibility in UK and EU law is not inherently progressive, as the legal scholars Diamond Ashiagbor and Sandra Fredman have shown.[5] The 'promise' of flexible work does not fit with the working conditions of a vast number of women and should no longer dominate government solutions to gender inequality in the workplace.

Women in precarious jobs interviewed for this study worked as cleaners, care-workers, nurses, supermarket workers, other types of retail workers, teachers, lecturers, administrators and researchers. Their jobs often did not fit the categories assumed in government guidance on flexible working. The government website explaining the right to request flexible work lists types of flexible work as including:

---

[4] Institute of Employment Rights (2016) 'Manifesto for Labour Law', fn 2, this chapter.

[5] Ashiagbor, D. (2006) *The European Employment Strategy: Labour Market Regulation and New Governance*, Oxford: Oxford University Press; Fredman, S. (2004) chapter 1, fn 19.

- job sharing
- working from home
- part time
- compressed hours
- flexitime
- annualized hours
- staggered hours[6]

Many of the women interviewed for this study would not have been able to work flexibly in these ways because the types of jobs they did required them to be present in the workplace and were structured by employers to fit their own wider organizational systems. Working from home is impossible in care, cleaning and retail settings, as Tina pointed out in the excerpt from her interview at the beginning of this chapter. Part-time work and compressed hours are not necessarily flexible and often do not fit nursery and school opening times, as we have seen in Chapter Four. For example, both Kelly and Fiona had what were effectively compressed part-time jobs, but these did not provide them with sufficient income or with the hours they needed in order to be able to manage care easily. Annualized hours and staggered hours presume a high degree of worker autonomy, which again is often not present in precarious jobs in retail, care, cleaning and education.

A further problem with this paradigm is that in requiring employees to make a request for flexible work, it ignores any imbalance of bargaining power in the workplace. This is enough of a problem for people with secure employment status, but for precarious workers it is even more exclusionary because, as we have seen, women on precarious contracts interviewed for this study feared reprisals and did not want to "rock the boat". While some level of communication between worker and employer is necessary to ensure care-friendly work patterns, using a model whereby

---

[6]   See https://www.gov.uk/flexible-working/types-of-flexible-working

flexible work must be negotiated without also taking action to address imbalances in bargaining power is likely to fail precarious workers.

For this reason, rights for precarious workers and others should move away the paradigm of flexible work and draw instead on a paradigm of care-friendly work. Such rights should be suitable for those employed in a wide range of working contexts, including care, retail, cleaning, hospitality and transport, in which the worker is required to be present. Precarious workers should have rights that are clear, accessible and universal so as to counter the intense imbalance of bargaining power that these workers face. Such rights should avoid reliance on individual negotiation, in which workers can be overpowered by managers.

Focus first on the care responsibility

The usual approach with family-friendly employment rights has been to start with the employment relationship. Employees have been given preferential treatment in family-friendly rights and this means that people need to know whether they are an employee in order to know many of their legal rights. Having to focus on the type of label someone has at work ('employee', 'worker') distracts us from the type of care they are providing and the wider social benefit this care brings. The women interviewed for this study put considerable time, ingenuity, financial resources and emotional effort into providing care for children and adults in arrangements that went beyond the Western nuclear family norm. They did this because no matter what type of employment status they had, the care needed to happen and the responsibility had fallen to them. As Dipika put it:

'Caring is a public duty. It's my responsibility. I take it on willingly. I do it unpaid. It makes a difference to the community that my kids aren't feral (laughs)'.

As many have pointed out, including women interviewed for this study, this unpaid care is extremely valuable financially and of much wider social benefit:

> 'People like me that do the caring at home, we save the government ... millions of pounds, and get nothing in return'. (Sam, supermarket worker)

For rights to care-friendly working to be meaningful, we should start by recognizing this care work and base our legal response on its social value.[7] We should begin with the recognition that a person is doing unpaid care, instead of asking whether that person is an employee. In a legal system that respects the value of unpaid care, we should not have to ask whether someone is an employee or a worker before they are given rights to manage care alongside work.

Increase access to paid leave

Women reported struggling with fluctuating incomes, and described having to pay strict attention to budgets in order to 'make ends meet'. In this context, their ability to draw on rights to unpaid leave – for example, the right to time off to care for family and dependents, or so called 'emergency leave' – was compromised. In some circumstances, women resorted to stating that they were "off sick" in order to avoid having their pay 'docked' for an emergency care situation. It should not be necessary for women to consider doing this. In view of the considerable economic benefit provided by women's unpaid care, government should ensure that women do not miss out on income when performing care. At the very least, access to paid leave in emergencies should be available to all workers.

---

[7] Nicole Busby has proposed such an approach in relation to European employment law. See Busby, N. (2011) *A Right to Care: Unpaid Care Work in European Employment Law*, Oxford: Oxford University Press.

Ensure rights from day one

Many family-friendly employment rights have qualifying periods, a period of time starting at the outset of employment during which an employee cannot draw on certain rights. Ironically, this includes the right to request flexible work and rights to maternity and paternity pay, despite such periods having been previously found to constitute an unlawful form of sex discrimination, as Lizzie Barmes has discussed.[8] Qualifying periods create an unprotected zone of employment just when someone starts a new job, which is exactly the time when they are settling into the role, might feel less able to negotiate for care-friendly work and could benefit from statutory rights. Furthermore, qualifying periods prevent some people on very short term contracts from ever being able to use their rights, even if they are otherwise eligible. Care-friendly rights for precarious workers should not include any qualifying periods.[9] These rights should recognize that when someone with a care responsibility takes on a new job, their care continues and they should be protected from day one of their employment.

Do not leave it to workers to enforce their rights

In each job, employers determine the expectations associated with the role, as well as the working hours and shift patterns.

---

[8]   See Barmes, L. (1996) 'Public Law, EC Law and the Qualifying Period for Unfair Dismissal', *Industrial Law Journal*, 25(1): 59–61.

[9]   Most recently, this has been recommended by the House of Commons Women & Equalities Committee in their 2021 report *Unequal Impact? Coronavirus and the gendered economic impact*. See also: Institute of Employment Rights (2016) 'Manifesto for Labour Law'; and TUC (2019) 'Good Work Plan: Proposals to Better Support Families, TUC Response to BEIS Consultation', available at: https://www.tuc.org.uk/sites/default/files/2019-12/TUC_BEISConsultation_GoodWorkPlan.pdf; and Working Families (2013) 'Children and Families Bill – Second Reading Briefing'. Copy on file with author.

The current paradigm for enforcing family-friendly rights in UK employment law is to require an employee or worker to make a claim in an employment tribunal after taking certain steps, including early conciliation through ACAS (Advisory, Conciliation and Arbitration Service). This puts the onus on the employee or worker to resolve problems at work, which can be intimidating, time consuming and expensive, as Nicole Busby, Morag McDermont and Emily Rose have shown.[10] Where the imbalance of bargaining power between worker and employer is particularly stark, as we have seen is the case with many women balancing precarious work and care, the current tribunal method of enforcement is particularly inappropriate.

The Equality and Human Rights Commission (EHRC) has powers to monitor employers and take enforcement action where an employment issue relating to a care responsibility engages the Equality Act 2010. This includes specific powers if the employer is a public body subject to the Public Sector Equality Duty. The EHRC could be encouraged to assess how it can use its powers to further research and protect the position of women in precarious work with unpaid care responsibilities.

Another approach would be to create an official enforcement system for care-friendly rights, with the power to investigate employers and bring civil proceedings on behalf of a worker or a group of workers if an employer does not facilitate care-friendly work. The Institute of Employment Rights' 'Manifesto for Labour Law' proposed an independent labour inspectorate which would have the power to enter workplaces, issue enforcement notices and bring legal proceedings against employers. Giving such an inspectorate a specific remit to investigate employers' approaches to facilitating unpaid care

---

[10] See Busby, N. and McDermont, M. (2020) 'Fighting With the Wind: Claimants' Experiences and Perceptions of the Employment Tribunal', *Industrial Law Journal*, 49(2): 159–98; Rose, E. and Busby, N. (2017) 'Power Relations in Employment Disputes', *Journal of Law & Society*, 44(4): 674–701.

for all workers would help redress the imbalance of bargaining power between employers and workers.

Conclusion

The current structure of family-friendly employment rights is the result of a set of choices made by previous governments to exclude women in precarious work from many types of legal protection. This has to change. In this book, I have explored the experiences and strategies of women balancing precarious work and care. I have shown how these women's daily routines of care, and their care networks, are shaped around the changing requirements of precarious jobs, with far-reaching consequences for them and their loved ones. Yet the care that women provide, unpaid, for others, is often invisible to employers, who not only determine the types of contracts available to workers but also often fail to ensure that their organizational patterns are care friendly. The employment rights normally available to employees are rarely available to women in precarious work, who instead draw conclusions about their ability to disclose care or negotiate flexible work based on what they understand of their contracts. In the current context of the COVID-19 pandemic, the increasing use of zero-hours contracts, the rise of the 'gig economy' and widespread use of agency work, it is unacceptable that the dominant paradigm for family-friendly working is that of an employee in a secure, professional, office-based job making a request for flexible work. Valuing the unpaid care that women provide means valuing all women workers, no matter what kind of job or contract they have. The time has come to provide care-friendly rights for precarious workers.

Appendix: How the Research Was Conducted

This report draws on in-depth interviews conducted with 33 women from across the mainland UK, and on legal research into family-friendly employment rights. The research explored two core questions:

1. What are the experiences of women who balance unpaid care with precarious work?
2. To what extent does current UK employment law recognize those experiences?

'Precarious work' is defined in this project as:

A. work that falls outside of the 'standard employment relationship' or model due to length or type of contract (for instance, temporary or 'zero-hours' contracts), **or**
B. work that is precarious for another reason identified by an interview respondent, including institutional factors concerning the structure and allocation of work through organizations (for example, a long-term, very short hours, permanent contract in a supermarket exposing the worker to insufficient pay and restricted career development).

Interviews

Interviews were conducted between June 2015 and January 2017 and aimed to capture women's experiences of balancing precarious paid work alongside unpaid care obligations. Interviews were unstructured, with some prompts, and most lasted about an hour. Recruitment took place via emails and flyers distributed through advisory board contacts, snowballing, and via in-person approaches at legal advice centres (with the prior agreement of advice organizations). Recruitment strategies were altered throughout the study in response to sampling and monitoring of general uptake. Sampling took account of geographical location, type of work, type of contract, self-defined ethnicity, type of care obligation, educational attainment and parenting status.

Interviewees were all women with current or recent experience of precarious work and unpaid care living in the mainland UK (Dundee, Glasgow, Durham, York, Leeds, Liverpool, Stoke-on-Trent, Manchester, Nottingham, Milton Keynes, Ebbw Vale and London). Care obligations included care for dependent children, adults and those with disabilities. Most interviews were conducted in person, although some happened over telephone or Skype, and some were conducted as 'walking interviews'. Where possible, interviewees were asked to sketch their experiences of balancing care with precarious work. Supermarket vouchers were offered to interviewees as a thank you. Interviews were recorded and transcribed with the interviewees' permission, and anonymized transcripts were, when possible, sent to interviewees for their input prior to being analyzed. Interview transcripts are available through the United Kingdom Data Service's ReShare scheme.[1]

Interviewees

- Self-described ethnicity: White (13); Asian (5); Black British (3); Black (2); White British (2); African Caribbean (1); 'mixed race' (1); Brazilian (1); British Asian (1); Sri Lankan (1); Iranian (1); unknown (1).

---

[1] Catalogue number 853015. See further: https://www.ukdataservice.ac.uk/

- Contract: permanent part time/low hours (7); other part time (7); zero hours (3); casual (8); currently unemployed (3); multiple contracts (2); temporary or fixed term (6); agency (2).
- Sector/type: retail (9); further and higher education (8); care (7); cleaning (4); other public sector (3).
- Type of care: child (29); adult (15); disability (11).
- Parental status: lone (13); with another (19).
- Education: no formal (1); GCSEs (3); high school/A Levels (4); undergraduate university (7); postgraduate university (9); unknown (6).

Analysis

Interviews were analyzed in multiple phases. Early stages of analysis focused on descriptive information (for example, type of work contract, type of care, location, pay) and key themes bearing on the research (for instance, knowledge of workers' own contracts, knowledge of family-friendly rights). Later stages picked up on emerging themes (the effect of last minute shifts on care arrangements, willingness to negotiate flexible work and so forth) and traced women's own narratives of issues in their lives such as career history, daily routines and hopes for the future.

Some themes suggested new lines of legal research fairly early on. For example, the practice of women taking sick leave to cover a care emergency emerged as a theme and this led to legal research on the position of workers with a range of contracts with respect to sick leave and pay, as well as on potential disciplinary action for using leave other than for sickness.

The final stages of analysis involved cross-referencing significant themes in the three core areas of knowledge of law, care strategies and work strategies reflected in this book with current employment rights to understand the extent to which the law recognizes widespread experiences among women balancing precarious work with unpaid care.

During the course of the research, analytic strategies and interim findings were presented and tested in a number of ways, including:

- presentations at academic conferences and seminars: Universities of Kent and Oxford, 2013; Labour Law Research Network, 2013; staff seminars at Universities of Birmingham (2015), Leeds (2016) and Osgoode Hall Law School, Toronto (2015); Socio-Legal Studies Association conference (2018); Society of Legal Scholars conference (2018);
- the launch of an interim report at a 'brainstorming day' held at Friend's House, London in June 2016 and attended by interviewees, trade unions and NGOs from the UK and Canada (including the Workers' Action Centre, Toronto) – participants were invited to give feedback on the interim report and make suggestions for the later stages of the research;
- a dedicated interdisciplinary workshop of academics researching labour regulation: 'Social studies of labour regulation', University of Kent, June 2016;
- updating meetings with the TUC, Working Families and USDAW (Union of Shop, Distributive and Allied Workers);
- a collaborative analysis day hosted by USDAW in March 2017. Key themes from analysis were identified and anonymized interview data relating to the themes were provided for consideration. USDAW women's representatives from around the UK helped assess the direction of analysis and gave feedback on their own understanding of how the interview data related to their own, and their members', experiences of balancing work and care;
- presentation of key findings to NGOs, trade unions and Government Equality Office experts at the Working Families 'Families and Work' Group, July 2019.

Index

Page numbers in *italic* type refer to figures.
References to footnotes show both the
page number and the note number (231n3).

Printed and bound by CPI Group (UK) Ltd, Croydon, CR0 4YY

25/03/2025

14647336-0003